D1168382

wise
COCKTAILS

wise COCKTAILS

The Owl's Brew Guide to
CRAFTING & BREWING
TEA-BASED BEVERAGES

JENNIE RIPPS & MARIA LITTLEFIELD
Founders of Owl's Brew

Photographs by Tina Rupp

RODALE.

© 2015 by Jennie Ripps and Maria Littlefield

Rodale books may be purchased for business or promotional use or for special sales. For information, please write to:
Special Markets Department, Rodale Inc.,
733 Third Avenue, New York, NY 10017

Printed in the United States of America
Rodale Inc. makes every effort to use acid-free ♾, recycled paper ♻.

Photo credits: Nicole Franzen (page xi) and Grant Monahan (page xiv)

Illustration credits: Marco Govel/Shutterstock (chalkboard throughout); Kaitlin Bostwick (owl-approved stamp, page xiv); Sophia Chang (tipsy owl on chapter openers and page 96); art_of_sun/Shutterstock (paint swashes on pages 9, 24, 26, and 102); and Renata Sviridova (3 icons, page 79)

Photographs by Tina Rupp
Food styling by Chelsea Zimmer
Prop styling by Sarah Cave
Book design by Rae Ann Spitzenberger

Library of Congress Cataloging-in-Publication Data
is on file with the publisher.

ISBN 978–1–62336–567–7

Distributed to the trade by Macmillan

2   4   6   8   10   9   7   5   3   1   hardcover

We inspire and enable people to improve their lives and the world around them.
rodalewellness.com

For Max, to whom
I will always toast.
—J.R.

To Martin, the
liquor to my tea.
—M.L.

CONTENTS

Dear Reader

>> This book is written for you: the aspiring mixologist, the awesome mom, the young professional, the cool uncle, the inspired foodie, the I-can't-make-cocktails dilettante, the college student (there are better things to drink than vodka-crans!). We've had an exceptional journey and an amazing adventure all while building a brand and mixing up fun cocktails. We hope that this book imparts some of the wonder we've felt while making boozy libations with a most proper base. The romantics among you can brew and pour into a teacup Prohibition-style; the healthiest can read up on all the antioxidants before imbibing. We warmly welcome you to our comprehensive, easy, and occasionally humorous guide for how to brew and craft our favorite tea cocktails.

INTRODUCTION

Tea: A Love Story

Where do we begin? We could start with how we realized you could reap health benefits and stay hydrated while boozing; how you could stave off a hangover, craft some seriously delicious cocktails, and impress your friends by not serving up vodka-sodas all night long. We realized a lot of things about crafting tea for cocktails over the past several years. But *how* did it even start?

Well . . . like any good romance, it was love at first sight.

We—that is, Jennie and Maria—were colleagues at a boutique marketing firm. (Fun fact! Jennie actually hired Maria straight out of college. From intern to business partner. Sigh.) In the fall of 2011, we were managing some seriously high-profile events, working with lifestyle brands, wrangling celebrities, arranging venues, pitching sponsorships, coordinating programs surrounding Fashion Week, Sundance, Art Basel, the Super Bowl, polo events in the Hamptons,

Jennie

Maria

intimate events at Malibu beach houses, and so much more. Fun, for sure, but all of which made us feel crazy enough to pull our hair out at any given moment. In truth, we constantly needed a cup of tea to calm down—and then a stiff drink to take the edge off. Little did we know we'd soon be marrying the two and creating our very own company!

It all began with the simple beauty of tea itself: a sneaky little ingredient with endless possibilities. When you drop dried herbs and plants into water, you end up with something that tastes—well—like *something*. If you place dried ginger in water—not even hot water, but cool water(!)—for 10 minutes, you have a gingery libation. If you drop dried hibiscus into ambient-temperature water for 5 minutes, you have a glass of tart goodness in front of you. And if you combine these herbs, spices, and teas in a way that *might* be delicious . . . well, you end up with a whole lot more.

And then, of course, the health benefits. When green tea is placed in water—hot or cold—you brew up an antioxidant machine, with metabolism-boosting properties. Add some peppermint and you have a focus-promoting powerhouse. Throw in vanilla, and you get (ta-da!) mood-boosting properties.

Jennie went first, diving headlong into the allure of tea and the healing properties of leaves, herbs, and dried fruits: Who knew that cinnamon was anti-inflammatory, that cloves were a huge boost to the immune system, that sencha was jam-packed with free radical–fighting antioxidants?! In the winter of 2011, she launched our very first tea-fueled endeavor: Brew Lab Tea, specializing in custom-crafting delicious, unique, healthy tea blends for some of the most fantastic restaurants in NYC.

Brew Lab Tea's focus is on the nitty-gritty, real-deal, healthful properties of tea, and tea alone: It's about flavor and function. Three years ago, we chose a (wise) owl for our logo to drive home the point that you should know what you are putting into your body.

But we're pretty fun (we think), so it wasn't long after Brew Lab Tea was born that Jennie approached Maria about tea parties—and we're not talking about scones. Together, we made the jump from holding one glass of delish iced lemon verbena in our left hand and a cocktail in the other to what is now an obvious mash-up. Hello!? Mix 'em together!

What can we say? A star was born. Why wouldn't tea, this amazing product with a million flavor profiles and tons of brewy goodness, pair perfectly with spirits? And who said we needed to use sugary juices and sodas in our cocktails anyway?

In the early spring, we started hosting tea parties at the brownstone we worked out of. Twice a month, we'd invite our friends and family, and serve them seven or eight tea cocktails, usually crafted around a theme. Our Valentine's Day post-mortem party featured drinks such as If You Like Piña Coladas, My Bloody Valentine, and Cupid's Arrow. These tea parties were for fun, but we were really driven by something else: We wanted to know if people would love tea cocktails as much as we did. Many Tea-quila Poppers and Bloody Marias later, we were sure they did. And we realized that tea cocktails were super-easy to make (and drink!).

After that, it was a tea- and boozy-tea-fueled whirlwind. We were crafting cocktails and hitting events to pour 'em faster than you can say "matcha." Movie premieres, film festivals, fashion shows—you name it. Of course, we were fresh-brewing, on-site. This meant showing up with bags and bags of tea leaves and mixing them with water at events. This led to some rather . . . interesting . . . situations. It's hard to travel with several pounds of dried green tea leaves without looking like you're up to no good, if you catch our drift. . . .

For two years, we spent the first hour of any event scrambling for water sources and raging against the automatic sinks of the world. We fantasized about opening a bottle and simply pouring. While we nervously watched our bags come off the baggage claim, looking cautiously for telltale agave trickles on the carousel, we imagined a day when we wouldn't need to bubble-wrap our sweetener.

These yearnings made us even more determined to launch a product that was ready-to-pour. We did it for YOU, of course. But really—we did it for us.

In the summer of 2013, after some serious soul-searching and sink-searching (we can't tell you how many events we served at where they said they'd have accessible faucets for us to brew our tea in and then just didn't), we launched Owl's Brew, the first-ever bottled tea "crafted for cocktails." Owl's Brew is fresh brewed (we refuse to work with flavors or from concentrate), and each of our blends is made to pair with a variety of liquors, as well as beer, wine, and champagne.

This book is a compilation of everything we've learned about how to make delicious tea-based cocktails. We're giving you the scoop on how tea is made; a guide to some tools of the trade; and a tea-titillating and thoroughly unthorough guide to the history of tea. We've dabbled a bit in tea sodas and tea-infused foods, because . . . why the heck not?

Most of the cocktails are courtesy of yours truly. We've also had the honor of working with some seriously talented bartenders and chefs who have contributed their own cocktaily goodness.

We hope you have a glass in your hand. Drink Wise!

Cheers,
Jennie & Maria

CHAPTER 1

TOOLS,
TEAS
— & —
TISANES

*What You
Need to Know*

NOTES ON
BEVERAGES & TISANES

Brewing and infusing is how we make tea, but it doesn't just stop there. Gin contains a botanical bouquet—basically, an infusion of herbs and spices that almost always includes juniper in a spirit base. Bitters are made with gentian, citrus peels, and other ingredients. Grappa has a brandy (pomace) base made with grape skins, pulp, seeds, and stems, and is steeped with flavors ranging from orange to basil to fennel. Aquavit is a grain alcohol, often infused with caraway or dill. Even most sodas start off with brewing. You'll find brewed sarsaparilla in real root beer and ginger in old-fashioned ginger ale.

What we're tellin' ya is that one of the oldest—and most rewarding—traditions in this world is comprised of dropping fruits, herbs, spices, and a little good ol' *Camellia sinensis* into liquor or water. What's even better? Depending on how they're infused, and for how long, you derive a bushelful of health benefits. While we don't recommend drinking grappa to get your daily dose of vitamin C, we're still big proponents of the simple fact that using real stuff (not flavors or essences) is the best way to *drink wise. Santé!* To your health!

TEA TOOLS

Essential
* Cups
* Funnel
* Strainer
* Tea bags (black, white, green, rooibos)

Nonessential
(But Very Helpful)
* Dry-erase markers
* Kettle
* Large mason jar

* Linens
* Swing-top jar
* Tea ball
* Takeya iced tea makers

COCKTAIL TOOLS

Essential
* Agave nectar or raw sugar
* Shaker
* Stirrer

Nonessential
(But You'll Get a Lot Further)
* Citrus zester
* Colorful straws
* iSi whipper

* Jigger
* Knife
* Peeler
* Strainer
* Variety of glasses

Champagne
flute

Pilsner

Martini

Coupe

Rocks

GUIDE TO GLASSWARE

Wineglass

Collins

Highball

Heat-safe mug

THE HOME BAR

The Essentials

- Beer: amber ale, wheat beer, stout beer, IPA
- Bourbon/whiskey
- Champagne
- Gin
- Mezcal
- Spiced rum
- Tequila (white)
- Vodka
- Wine (red and white)
- White rum

The Fancy Home Bar

- Absinthe
- Aperol
- Bitters
- Brandy
- Campari
- Cocchi Americano
- Combier Original or Cointreau
- Créme de cassis
- Elderflower liqueur
- Ginger beer
- Ginger liqueur
- Grapefruit bitters
- Jenever
- Kahlúa
- Lillet
- Orange bitters
- Rye
- Sake
- Vermouth (sweet and dry)

COOKING TOOLS

- Baking sheet
- Garlic press
- Handheld blender
- Knives: chef's and paring
- Measuring cup
- Measuring spoons
- Saucepan
- Skillet
- Slotted spoon
- Soup pot

⸱⸳ TEA: THE PLANT ⸳⸱

We know our stuff, we promise. Here's our mini science lesson to prove it.

Tea is the second most consumed beverage in the world, following water. "Tea" as we know it can really be broken up into two categories. First is actual tea (black, green, and white), which is derived from the *Camellia sinensis* plant. Everything else commonly known as "tea" is an herb or botanical (e.g., chamomile, peppermint, lemon verbena).

In the wild, a tea plant may grow to be tree-size, but cultivated tea plants are pruned to shrub size. Botanists identify two primary varieties of the tea plant: *Camellia sinensis sinensis* and *Camellia sinensis assamica*. The *sinensis* variety is able to withstand brief periods of frost and can be grown at high altitudes—its infusions tend to be more delicate. The *assamica* cannot withstand frost—its larger leaves produce a high yield and more robust infusions.

Tea is a veritable treasure trove of health benefits. It includes vitamins B_2, C, and E; minerals such as potassium, manganese, folic acid, and calcium; and a wealth of antioxidants—in particular, tea is an excellent source of catechins, which protect against free radicals. Green tea has been very well studied, and its antioxidant level has been reported to be 100 times more effective than vitamins C and E in protecting our immune systems.

There are six kinds of teas made from the *Camellia sinensis* plant, although we only use the four most common teas for our delicious brews.

BLACK TEA

Black tea is the most processed of all teas, as it is fully oxidized. The fresh leaves are withered for a number of hours, and then rolled. After they have oxidized sufficiently, the leaves are heated and then dried in wood fires.

Typical preparation: Brew at 195° to 205°F for 3 to 5 minutes.

Famous Black Teas

* ✿ Assam
* ✿ Ceylon
* ✿ Darjeeling
* ✿ Keemun
* ✿ Lapsang Souchong *(this has a smoky flavor because of the pine wood fire used in the final drying process)*

GREEN TEA

Green tea is minimally oxidized—the leaves are usually withered but not rolled. Following the brief oxidation period, the leaves are steamed or pan-fried to halt oxidation, and then rolled again.

Typical preparation: Brew at 170° to 180°F for 2 minutes.

Famous Green Teas

* ✿ Bancha
* ✿ Genmaicha
* ✿ Gunpowder
* ✿ Hyson & Young Hyson
* ✿ Matcha
* ✿ Sencha

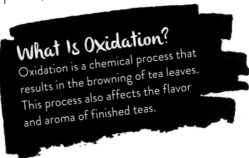

What Is Oxidation?

Oxidation is a chemical process that results in the browning of tea leaves. This process also affects the flavor and aroma of finished teas.

People often ask us how much tea to use per cup. Our answer is: a <u>teaspoon</u>! It's true—the use of teaspoons dates back to 1600s England, and to this day, is the right measurement for the perfect cuppa.

WHITE TEA

White tea is the least processed of all teas, and the leaves are not oxidized. White tea gets its color because only the top leaves and immature buds are picked.

Typical preparation: Brew at 170° to 180°F for 2 to 3 minutes.

Famous White Teas

* Silver Needle
* White Peony or Pai Mu Tan
* Darjeeling White

OOLONG TEA

Oolong teas are processed similarly to black teas—they are withered and then rolled or shaken; however, oolongs are only oxidized for about half the time of typical black teas.

Typical preparation: Brew at 195° to 205°F for 3 to 6 minutes.

Famous Oolong Teas

* Wuyi Rock Oolong from the Fujian Province
* Ti Kuan Yin
* Pouchong
* Formosa Oolong

The Power of the Leaf

LEAVES OF FRUIT, WHEN BREWED, OFTEN HAVE MEDICINAL benefits. For instance, when we brew a raspberry in tea, we are left with loads of vitamin C and polyphenols. When we add raspberry leaves into the mix, we get an even higher concentration of vitamin C as well as magnesium and B vitamins. Other leaves, such as strawberry and blueberry, have similar superpowers!

TISANES & HERBS

Botanicals, spices, and flowers are all tisanes. While not technically tea, these bitter, spicy, savory, and sweet add-ins contain a wealth of nutrients and offer unique flavors. We've highlighted the health benefits of some of our favorites, which you will find commonly used in our recipes, particularly in the DIY chapter (page 28).

BASIL is a botanical super-star, containing vitamins A, C, and K and even zinc, iron, and chlorophyll. It's also rich in antioxidants, and relieves stress.

BLACK PEPPER spurs digestion, aids in weight loss, and has antibacterial properties.

CARDAMOM is rich in vitamins A and C and contains iron and zinc. It is a natural anti-inflammatory and is traditionally used as an aphrodisiac.

CHAMOMILE promotes calm and provides full-body stress relief; it is also excellent for soothing an upset stomach.

CLOVES are rich in manganese, among other antioxidants, and stabilize the nervous system. On a detox? Cloves freshen the breath and help the body metabolize fat.

GINGER has natural anti-nausea properties and can help relieve an upset stomach; it is also a great immunity booster.

HIBISCUS FLOWERS are natural anti-inflammatories. Hibiscus tea is rich in antioxidants, is excellent for respiratory health, and is often used as a sleep aid.

JASMINE FLOWERS naturally remove toxins from the body. Additionally, they are believed to have aphrodisiac properties, and are natural stress reducers.

LAVENDER is a calming tisane that can help alleviate restlessness, insomnia, and anxiety. It also has properties that aid digestion.

LEMONGRASS has natural detoxifying properties and helps promote a healthy complexion.

PEELS (LEMON, ORANGE) Orange peel contains flavonoids and is rich in vitamin C—in fact, the peel is richer in vitamin C, vitamin A, and B complex vitamins than the fruit inside! Similarly, lemon peel contains at least five times more vitamins than lemon juice. These slightly bitter peels are excellent sources of fiber, potassium, magnesium, calcium, and beta-carotene.

PEPPERMINT is a natural, caffeine-free way to boost focus. It is also an anti-inflammatory and a particularly powerful stomach soother.

ROOIBOS is often called nature's sports drink. It contains natural electrolytes and minerals, including iron, potassium, and calcium. This African bush has anti-allergenic properties, is a natural anti-inflammatory, and is also rich in antioxidants.

ROSE PETALS are a natural source of vitamin C, can help ladies with pain at their time of the month, and are excellent for the complexion.

VANILLA promotes relaxation and reduces anxiety—and it's also a natural mood booster.

YERBA MATÉ is a loaded antioxidant powerhouse. It also promotes focus, aids in digestion, and, through its stimulant properties, enhances endurance.

Caffeine

APPROXIMATELY 80 PERCENT OF THE CAFFEINE IN TEA IS RELEASED during the first 30 seconds of steeping. Therefore, to remove most of the caffeine from any tea, simply follow this procedure:

1 Pour boiling water over the tea leaves.

2 Steep the leaves for 30 seconds.

3 Pour out the water, saving the steeped leaves.

4 Resteep the same leaves in fresh boiling water for the recommended steeping time.

. . . OR TRY THE COLD-BREW METHOD!

 Cold-brewed tea has one-half to two-thirds of the caffeine content of hot-brewed tea.

⁝ HOW TO BREW TEAS ⁝

Note: This is NOT our guide to brewing tea for cocktails! You'll find those instructions detailed in each DIY recipe. These are just our tips and tricks for brewing a delicious cuppa.

HOW TO HOT-BREW TEA

1. Measurement:
6 to 8 ounces water per
1 teaspoon tea.

2. Heat the water so it's
hot and steaming, but not
boiling (or, if you have a
way to heat it to the precise
recommended tempera-
tures detailed earlier in
the chapter—go for it!).

3. Timing:
✴ *Green or white tea
hot brews for 2 to
3 minutes.*

✴ *Black tea hot-brews
for 5 minutes.*

✴ *Tisanes hot-brew for
at least 5 minutes.*

✴ *If hot-brewing with a
blend that includes green
or white tea, allow those
teas to dictate the timing.*

4. If the tea leaves are
loose, strain them out
through a tea strainer; if
they are in a sachet, bag,
or ball, remove the sachet.

HOW TO COLD-BREW ICED TEA

1. Measurement:
6 to 8 ounces water per
2 teaspoons tea.

2. Use room-temperature
water, not cold water, to
brew.

3. Brew for about 10 minutes, agitating or stirring
from time to time.

4. If you are working with
loose leaves, strain them
out through a tea strainer.
Otherwise, remove the
sachet/bag/ball.

5. Pat yourself on the
back—one of the great
benefits of cold brewing
is that you minimize the
chance of over-brewing!

CHAPTER 2

THE
HISTORY
» OF «
TEA

*Abroad and
on the Home Front*

TEA ABROAD

The word *tea* comes from the Amoy (Chinese) word *t'e*. The Mandarin word for "tea" is *cha*, which became *ch'a* in Cantonese. Tea is called *chai* in India, Afghanistan, Persia, Russia, and Turkey and the Arabic word for tea is *shai*.

The Dutch East India Company brought tea to Europe in 1610—first, Japanese green tea, and shortly after, Chinese tea. By 1637, tea, or *thee* as the Dutch called it, was the fashionable drink in the Dutch capital, The Hague. By the 1640s, Holland's primary tea customers were the Frisians of what is now northwest Germany.

The Dutch influence even extended to the British—the future Charles II (r. 1660–1685) was introduced to tea during his exile in The Hague, while his Portuguese wife, Catherine of Braganza, is largely credited with bringing tea into England.

By 1658, the first advertisement for tea appeared in a London newspaper, and Samuel Pepys, the famous diarist, drank his first cup of tea on September 25, 1660. In Queen Anne's reign, in the early 1700s, the nobility "scandalously" started substituting tea for ale at breakfast, and in 1706, Thomas Twining opened the city's first teahouse, where ladies (banned from coffeehouses) could purchase tea.

London's famous tea gardens, such as the Vauxhall Gardens, provided a destination for the entire family. There were diversions, including performances where music could be enjoyed. Hot chocolate, coffee, and, of course, tea were served.

By the early 1700s, the British appetite for tea was so pronounced that an entire trade was built around "fake" tea, also known as *smouch*. This adulterated tea first appeared in the market in the mid-1720s, and by 1777, it was estimated that approximately 2 million pounds of various leaves and wood were being added to 12 million pounds of tea annually.

Between 1801 and 1911, official tea imports increased more than tenfold, from 23.7 million pounds to 295.3 million pounds, while the average price of tea fell, due to the capacity and efficiency of new clipper and steamer ships. This thirst for tea played a role in rituals and tradition—according to British tea lore, the institution of afternoon tea was invented by the Duchess of Bedford in the mid-1840s. She experienced a "sinking feeling" in the late afternoon, and commissioned tea served with cakes and snacks around 5:00 p.m. She began inviting friends to join her, and soon afternoon tea (or low tea) became a convivial ritual in middle- and upper-class households. High tea, which is now associated with the tea ceremony, was actually a working-class meal, served on a high table at the end of the workday. High tea service was accompanied by a hearty meal that often included meat dishes as well as baked goods and cheese.

Tea cocktails and punches were not that common in the UK, but in 1930, in *The Savoy Cocktail Book* by Harry Craddock, green tea makes an appearance in Milk Punch (No. 1), which also includes cloves, coriander, pineapple, and milk.

Later in this classic book, Mr. Craddock names a section Cocktails Suitable for a Prohibition Country and includes the Mr. Manhattan Cocktail, a mint tisane–based cocktail.

A TIMELINE
→ OF TEA ←
in Europe

1610
The first shipment of tea reaches The Hague, and tea is fervently embraced by the Dutch.

1650
Tea appears in Germany.

1657
Dutch-traded Chinese tea is introduced in London as a health beverage.

1662
English king Charles II weds Princess Catherine of Braganza, an avid tea drinker.

1684
The British East India Company gains clearance from the Chinese to purchase tea directly and exclusively.

1723
Tea is first mentioned in Scandinavia.

1840s
The Duchess of Bedford experiences a "sinking feeling" in the afternoon and begins the ritual of afternoon tea.

1834
The monopoly of the British East India Company ends.

1865
Afternoon tea receptions are introduced at Buckingham Palace under the reign of Queen Victoria.

During the 18th century, both black and green teas were consumed in Britain, but by the early 1800s, there was a marked preference toward black tea.

ON THE HOME FRONT

Tea was initially brought to the Americas—and to our hometown of NYC—by the Dutch. Peter Stuyvesant, a Dutch governor, introduced the first tea to New Amsterdam in 1647. In the late 1600s, the famous Quaker William Penn brought tea with him to Philadelphia, which he founded on the Delaware River. In 1757, according to records, George Washington ordered six teapots and 12 pounds of tea.

THE TEA WATER MEN OF NYC

IN THE FIRST HALF OF THE 1700s, A SPRING OF FRESHWATER between Baxter Street and Mulberry Street became very desirable and was soon known as the tea water pump, as it was excellent for making tea. The tea water pump became a landmark of sorts and was often referred to in real estate deeds and indicated on maps.

In the 1740s, a delivery service sprang up around the pump, and tea water men with big casks would deliver water to subscribers. Eventually, a picnic area was built around it, known as the tea water pump garden.

Other tea water pumps were located on Chatham Street and at Knapp's Spring near Tenth Avenue and 14th Street. Water from the tea water pumps was delivered in NYC in such excess that traffic was often impeded. In 1757, the common council passed a law for the "regulating of tea water men in the city of New York."

Tea & the Prohibition

THE AMERICAN PROHIBITION HELPED BOOST THE popularity of iced tea—during this time, iced tea recipes began appearing regularly in Southern cookbooks.

At the same time, in the speakeasies of Chicago and New York, among others, liquor was disguised in teacups, in case of a raid.

Tea is inextricably interlaced with the history of the United States of America. Tea was so popular in colonial New York that at one time the small colony consumed more loose-leaf tea than all of England.

In particular, the Boston Tea Party (which left Boston Harbor awash in 90,000 pounds of tea) was one of the first salvos of the American Revolution. This event was spurred by colonists' outrage toward the British parliament's 1773 decision to allow the East India Company to highly tax tea for the American colonies.

After the Revolution, to get away from the British stranglehold, the Americans soon began importing tea from the Far East. By 1789, the American government was imposing its own tax on tea.

Tea continued to be popular in the United States in the 19th century. Early recipes for iced tea abound—the earliest sweet tea recipe in print comes from *Housekeeping in Old Virginia* by Marion Cabell Tyree, published in 1879.

Mrs. Tyree also included a recipe for Regent Punch, which included "One pint of strong black tea . . . one pint of French brandy, one pint of rum, two quarts of Champagne. Serve in a bowl, with plenty of ice."

Modern American Drinks, published in 1895, includes recipes for Tea Lemonade (the original Arnold Palmer!) as well as for various liquor-based tea punches.

Quite a few tea cocktail recipes appeared in both English and American cookbooks during the early 19th century. In *The Kentucky Housewife* (published in 1839), Mrs. Lettice Bryan included a recipe for Tea Punch. Served hot or cold, this called for a base of black tea (very strong), a loaf of sugar, and rich cream.

Jerry Thomas, an American bartender, published his famed *How to Mix Drinks: Or, The Bon-Vivant's Companion* in 1862 and in it he detailed multiple tea cocktails by number—#47 Nonsuch Punch, #87 Dry Punch, #81 Regent's Punch, and so on. In it, he states that #58 Royal Punch is "a composition worthy of a king." The recipe called for green tea, rum, brandy, curacao, and arrack. Mr. Thomas also included the "1 gill of warm calf's-foot jelly," prudently noting ". . . If the punch is too strong, add more green tea to taste."

Later, tea cocktails appear in 1895's *Modern American Drinks,* which describes both a Gin Tea Punch and a Tea Punch, Frappé (spiked with Jamaica rum).

CONTEMPORARY TEA COCKTAILS

Lucky for us (and for you!), we are currently in the midst of an excellent time for cocktails, and an even better one for tea.

Teas and botanicals are "having a moment," and the tea-based brews that bartenders around the country are cooking up are better than ever.

Let's say you find yourself at a terrific bar or lounge in Portland, or Seattle, or New York, or Chicago . . . there's a good chance that a tea-infused cocktail will be on the menu. Our advice? Try 'em all and mix 'em up at home, too!

From the classic and somewhat curious cocktails of the 19th century to the current trend of libations featuring fresh and dried herbs, it's pretty clear that tea is the perfect mixer: versatile, healthy, refreshing, and delicious.

Not convinced yet? Brew up some of our favorite blends, then sweeten, spike, and garnish—and let us know if we've changed your mind!

A SIDE NOTE ABOUT MIXOLOGY AND TEA

Bartenders have been using tea for years. Here's our crib sheet for the at-home entertainer hoping to work with teas and tisanes!

CHAPTER 3

DIY
TEA COCKTAIL
recipes

Tea-based cocktails offer a light, delicious, and antioxidant-rich way to imbibe. Each tea is unique and gives your body a little boost, while offering a delicious complement to a variety of spirits, beers, and wines. Best of all, our yummy tea-based cocktails are hydrating and low in sugar.

In other words—booze with benefits! Sip pretty!

A NOTE ON DRIED INGREDIENTS VERSUS FRESH INGREDIENTS

In these recipes, we have provided instructions for using (mostly) dried fruits and spices. However, if you don't have these on hand—or can't find them—swap the dried ingredients for fresh—or common—ones. For example, you can chop up fresh basil instead of dried, or try a drop of vanilla extract instead of dried vanilla. Any fresh ingredients will add an extra boost of flavor, so portion accordingly! Most important, you can't mess this up—all the cocktails you make are going to be delicious. Feel free to go off-map a little and mix up your own superstar tea cocktails.

ABOUT OUR BREWING INSTRUCTIONS

We have included a step-by-step process with each recipe for how to cold-brew your tea cocktail bases. We love cold brewing, because you don't run the risk of over-brewing, and your fabulous cocktails will chill that much faster.

We always say to stir or dry-shake (dry-shaking is simply using a shaker without ice). The reason you shouldn't shake our DIY blends with ice is that tea is delicate, and a lot of shaking will quickly dilute the cocktails.

WHITE MULE

An antioxidant-loaded tea base.

• • • • • • ' • • ' • ' • • ' • • • • • • • • • • • • •

TEA BASE
1 teaspoon white
tea leaves

½ teaspoon chopped
lemongrass

½ teaspoon dried
peach

COCKTAIL
3½ oz brewed
tea base

1½ oz vodka

¾ tablespoon agave
nectar

3 oz ginger beer

GARNISH
1 fresh ginger slice

*Makes 1
cocktail*

In a cup, place 5 oz of room temperature water. You will only use 3½ oz for the tea base in this recipe, so don't worry if there is extra left over. Feel free to sip, save, or discard!

In a tea linen or tea ball, combine all the ingredients for the tea base. Brew in the room temperature water for 10 minutes, agitating from time to time. Remove the sachet/ball.

In a shaker, combine 3½ oz of the tea base, the vodka, and the agave nectar. Dry-shake until the agave dissolves. Pour into a glass over ice and gently swirl to chill. Top with the ginger beer and gently swirl again. Garnish with the ginger slice.

WHITE ARNOLD

White tea is complemented by clarifying and energizing lemon peel. Strawberries and rose petals add a boost of vitamin C.

TEA BASE
1 teaspoon white tea leaves

½ teaspoon rose petals

½ teaspoon dried strawberries

Pinch of dried lemon peel

COCKTAIL
4½ oz brewed tea base

1½ oz vodka

1 tablespoon agave nectar

GARNISH
1 lemon slice

Makes 1 cocktail

In a cup, place 6 oz of room temperature water. You will only use 4½ oz for the tea base in this recipe, so don't worry if there is extra left over. Feel free to sip, save, or discard!

In a tea linen or tea ball, combine all of the ingredients for the tea base. Brew in the room temperature water for 10 minutes, agitating from time to time. Remove the sachet/ball.

In a shaker, combine 4½ oz of the tea base, the vodka, and agave nectar. Dry-shake until the agave dissolves. Pour into a glass over ice. Gently swirl to chill. Garnish with the lemon slice.

For a strawberry punch: Add 2 fresh strawberries to the shaker and muddle. Then add the tea base, vodka, and agave, and dry-shake. Serve over ice.

THE NEW GIRL

The energizing and caffeine-free tea base contains mood-boosting lemongrass and focus-promoting peppermint.

TEA BASE
1 teaspoon chopped lemongrass

1 teaspoon dried peppermint

COCKTAIL
4 oz brewed tea base

1½ oz vodka

½ oz lavender simple syrup

Dash of lemon juice

GARNISH
1 fresh sprig lavender

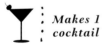
Makes 1 cocktail

In a cup, place 6 oz of room temperature water. You will only use 4 oz for the tea base in this recipe, so don't worry if there is extra left over. Feel free to sip, save, or discard!

In a tea linen or tea ball, combine the lemongrass and peppermint. Brew in the room temperature water for 10 minutes, agitating from time to time. Remove the sachet/ball.

In a shaker, combine 4 oz of the tea base, the vodka, simple syrup, and lemon juice. Dry-shake so that all the ingredients are well mixed, and then add ice to the shaker. Gently swirl to chill. Pour into a glass. Garnish with the lavender sprig.

COUNT ON ME

Fresh and light, this cocktail is a perfect summer sipper. Rooibos is loaded with electrolytes to keep you hydrated on those hot days, and the berries and rose petals are chock-full of vitamin C and rich in antioxidants.

TEA BASE
1 teaspoon rooibos

¼ teaspoon rose petals

Mix together in equal parts and use 1 teaspoon:
Dried raspberries

Dried blueberries

Dried strawberries

COCKTAIL
4½ oz brewed tea base

1½ oz vodka

½ tablespoon agave nectar

½ oz rose simple syrup

GARNISH
Fresh raspberries

In a cup, place 6 oz of room temperature water. You will only use 4½ oz for the tea base in this recipe, so don't worry if there is extra left over. Feel free to sip, save, or discard!

In a tea linen or tea ball, combine all of the ingredients for the tea base. Brew in the room temperature water for 10 minutes, agitating from time to time. Remove the sachet/ball.

In a shaker, combine 4½ oz of the tea base, the vodka, agave nectar, and rose syrup. Dry-shake until the agave dissolves. Add ice to the shaker and swirl gently to chill. Pour into a glass and garnish with the fresh raspberries.

Makes 1 cocktail

This is our good friend's favorite cocktail, and her 8-year-old daughter was always trying to steal sips of her "adult" version, so she now pours her daughter her very own mocktail (before she adds the vodka, of course!).

THE PROHIBITION CLASSIC

Kick back with a classic. Calming lavender eases tension and aids the immune system, while the Earl Grey provides a minimal amount of energizing caffeine.

TEA BASE
1½ teaspoons Earl Grey tea leaves

½ teaspoon dried lavender

COCKTAIL
4 oz brewed tea base

1½ oz vodka

½ oz elderflower liqueur

GARNISH
1 lemon slice

 Makes 1 cocktail

In a cup, place 6 oz of room temperature water. You will only use 4 oz for the tea base in this recipe, so don't worry if there is extra left over. Feel free to sip, save, or discard!

In a tea linen or tea ball, combine the Earl Grey tea and lavender. Brew in the room temperature water for 10 minutes, agitating from time to time. Remove the sachet/ball.

In a shaker, combine 4 oz of the tea base, the vodka, and elderflower liqueur. Dry-shake gently. Strain and pour into a glass over ice. Swirl gently to chill. Garnish with the lemon slice.

THE NAKED ARNOLD

This tea cocktail first debuted at a photo shoot for
Vogue magazine in 2012. It's a vitamin C–rich brew
with the flavor profile of an Arnold Palmer.

TEA BASE
1 teaspoon Assam
tea leaves

1 teaspoon dried
strawberries

Pinch of dried
lemon peel

Pinch of strawberry
leaf

COCKTAIL
4½ oz brewed
tea base

1½ oz vodka

1 tablespoon agave
nectar

GARNISH
Fresh strawberries

In a cup, place 6 oz of room temperature water. You will only use 4½ oz
for the tea base in this recipe, so
don't worry if there is extra left over.
Feel free to sip, save, or discard!

In a tea linen or tea ball, combine
all of the ingredients for the tea base.
Brew in the room temperature water
for 10 minutes, agitating from time
to time. Remove the sachet/ball.

In a shaker, combine 4½ oz of the tea
base, the vodka, and agave nectar.
Dry-shake until the agave dissolves.
Pour into a glass over ice and swirl
gently to chill. Garnish with the
fresh strawberries.

Makes 1
cocktail

COCORANGE

This blend promotes calm and is a natural mood enhancer.

. . . . . ' , , , . ' . ' , ...

TEA BASE
1 teaspoon chopped lemongrass

½ teaspoon dried orange peel

½ teaspoon unsweetened shredded coconut

COCKTAIL
3½ oz brewed tea base

1½ oz vodka

1 oz pineapple juice

1 tablespoon agave nectar

GARNISH
1 pineapple slice

In a cup, place 6 oz of room temperature water. You will only use 3½ oz for the tea base in this recipe, so don't worry if there is extra left over. Feel free to sip, save, or discard!

In a tea linen or tea ball, combine all of the ingredients for the tea base. Brew in the room temperature water for 10 minutes, agitating from time to time. Remove the sachet/ball.

In a shaker, combine 3½ oz of the tea base, the vodka, pineapple juice, and agave nectar. Dry-shake until the agave dissolves. Pour into a glass over ice. Swirl gently to chill. Garnish with the pineapple slice.

 Makes 1 cocktail

THE SPEAKEASY SPECIAL

This blend calms the nervous system and improves digestion.

• • • • • ✎ ✎ ✎ ✎ ✎ ✎ • ✎ ✎ • • • • • • • • • • • •

TEA BASE
1 teaspoon dried lemon verbena

1 teaspoon ground ginger

COCKTAIL
3 oz brewed tea base

½ oz ginger liqueur

3 oz Prosecco

Makes 1 cocktail

In a cup, place 6 oz of room temperature water. You will only use 3 oz for the tea base in this recipe, so don't worry if there is extra left over. Feel free to sip, save, or discard!

In a tea linen or tea ball, combine the lemon verbena and ginger. Brew in the room temperature water for 10 minutes, agitating from time to time. Remove the sachet/ball.

In a shaker, combine 3 oz of the tea base and the ginger liqueur. Dry-shake to combine. Add ice and stir gently to chill. Strain and pour into a glass. Top with the Prosecco and swirl.

First served at a real-deal speakeasy on Manhattan's Lower East Side . . . sshh, we can't tell!

BERRY ROYALE

This berry-based blend is rich in vitamins and minerals.

TEA BASE
¼ teaspoon whole cloves

Mix together in equal parts and use 1¾ teaspoons:
Dried raspberries

Dried blueberries

Dried strawberries

COCKTAIL
3 oz brewed tea base

½ oz crème de cassis

3 oz Champagne

GARNISH
Fresh raspberries

 Makes 1 cocktail

In a cup, place 6 oz of room temperature water. You will only use 3 oz for the tea base in this recipe, so don't worry if there is extra left over. Feel free to sip, save, or discard!

In a tea linen or tea ball, combine all of the ingredients for the tea base. Brew in the room temperature water for 10 minutes, agitating from time to time. Remove the sachet/ball.

In a shaker, combine 3 oz of the tea base and the crème de cassis. Dry-shake, then add ice and stir gently to chill. Strain and pour into a glass. Top with the Champagne and gently swirl again. Float the fresh raspberries on top.

 You can always swap out the dried berries for fresh!

CHOCOLATE ARROW

This festive sipper is loaded with antioxidants, and vanilla is a natural aphrodisiac. We love it as a Valentine's Day treat!

• • • • • ⁄ ⁄ ⁄ • ⁄ ⁄ • ⁄ • ⁄ • • • • • • • • • • • •

TEA BASE
Mix together in equal parts and use 2 full teaspoons:
Hojicha tea leaves

Unsweetened shredded coconut

Vanilla beans

Dried fig (diced)

Chai spices (cinnamon, cardamom, ginger, nutmeg, cloves)

COCKTAIL
3 oz brewed tea base

1 oz Kahlúa

1 tablespoon agave nectar

3 oz Champagne

In a cup, place 6 oz of room temperature water. You will only use 3 oz for the tea base in this recipe, so don't worry if there is extra left over. Feel free to sip, save, or discard!

In a tea linen or tea ball, combine all of the ingredients for the tea base. Brew in the room temperature water for 10 minutes, agitating from time to time. Remove the sachet/ball.

In a shaker, combine 3 oz of the tea base, the Kahlúa, and agave nectar. Dry-shake until the agave dissolves. Add ice to the shaker and gently swirl to chill. Pour into a glass. Add the Champagne and gently swirl again.

Makes 1 cocktail

≫ No vanilla bean? Use a dash of extract instead!

This drink was a hit at
a Valentine's dance
at NYC's Plaza Hotel.

VANILLA HOJICHA

Hojicha is a green tea that is roasted over charcoal. The perfect tea for all you coffee lovers.

• • • • • ‚ ‚ ‚ ‚ ‚ ‚ ‚ • ‚ ‚ ‚ • • • • • • • • • • •

TEA BASE
1 teaspoon hojicha tea leaves

½ teaspoon chopped vanilla bean

½ teaspoon ground ginger

COCKTAIL
3 oz brewed tea base

1 oz ginger liqueur

3 oz Champagne

Makes 1 cocktail

In a cup, place 6 oz of room temperature water. You will only use 3 oz for the tea base in this recipe, so don't worry if there is extra left over. Feel free to sip, save, or discard!

In a tea linen or tea ball, combine all of the ingredients for the tea base. Brew in the room temperature water for 10 minutes, agitating from time to time. Remove the sachet/ball.

In a shaker, combine 3 oz of the tea base and the ginger liqueur. Dry-shake to combine. Add ice and swirl gently to chill. Strain and pour into a glass. Top with the Champagne and swirl gently again.

For a spiced treat, we love serving up our Vanilla Hojicha cocktail with a side of Coconut Chai Rice Pudding!

Coconut Chai Rice Pudding

contributed by the chefs of Plated

The talented crew at Plated offer a weekly box of seasonal ingredients (for recipes you select) delivered right to your doorstep. Hello, amazing!

////////////// /// /// / /// /// / //////////

⅓ cup Arborio rice

¾ cup water

½ cup milk

1 bag coconut chai tea*

2½ tablespoons sugar

¼ cup coconut milk

1 tablespoon unsweetened shredded coconut

*You can also use a Masala chai tea bag, and then fill another linen with a sprinkle of unsweetened shredded coconut.

Serves 2

In a medium pot, combine the rice, water, milk, tea bag, and sugar. Bring to a boil over high heat, then reduce the heat to medium, cover the pot, and simmer, stirring frequently, until the rice is tender, about 20 minutes.

Add the coconut milk to the pot and simmer, uncovered, until creamy, about 5 minutes.

While the rice pudding cooks, add the coconut to a medium skillet over medium heat and toast until fragrant and light golden, about 3 minutes. Remove from the skillet.

Remove and discard the tea bag from the pudding. Divide the rice pudding evenly between 2 bowls and top with the toasted coconut. Serve warm or cold.

SPARKLING ROSÉ

The Sparkling Rosé is filled with nutrients, including iron, vitamin C, and calcium.

TEA BASE
1 teaspoon dried strawberries

1 teaspoon rose petals

Pinch of strawberry leaf*

COCKTAIL
3 oz brewed tea base

1 oz elderflower liqueur

3 oz Champagne

 Makes 1 cocktail

In a cup, place 6 oz of room temperature water. You will only use 3 oz for the tea base in this recipe, so don't worry if there is extra left over. Feel free to sip, save, or discard!

In a tea linen or tea ball, combine all the ingredients for the tea base. Brew in the room temperature water for 10 minutes, agitating from time to time. Remove the sachet/ball.

In a shaker, combine 3 oz of the tea base and the elderflower liqueur. Dry-shake to combine. Add ice and swirl gently to chill. Strain and pour into a glass. Top with the Champagne and swirl gently again.

*Strawberry leaf is a health-booster and doesn't affect flavor—if you can't find it, this cocktail will still be delightful.

A dear friend of Maria's brewed this up for a wedding shower—we heard the bride was glowing!

Our friend Ben swears
by our First Kiss—he actually
poured this for himself and his
girlfriend and then asked her
to marry him on the spot!
She said yes!

FIRST KISS

This blend is naturally hydrating, rich in minerals, and contains vitamin K.

TEA BASE
¾ teaspoon rooibos

¼ teaspoon dried basil

Mix together in equal parts and use 1 teaspoon:
Dried pomegranate

Dried strawberries

COCKTAIL
4½ oz brewed tea base

1½ oz tequila

1 tablespoon agave nectar

GARNISH
1 fresh basil leaf

Makes 1 cocktail

In a cup, place 6 oz of room temperature water. You will only use 4½ oz for the tea base in this recipe, so don't worry if there is extra left over. Feel free to sip, save, or discard!

In a tea linen or tea ball, combine all of the ingredients for the tea base. Brew in the room temperature water for 10 minutes, agitating from time to time. Remove the sachet/ball.

In a shaker, combine 4½ oz of the tea base, the tequila, and agave nectar. Dry-shake until the agave dissolves. Add ice and gently swirl to chill. Strain and pour into a glass. Garnish with the basil leaf.

≫ Sub in fresh pomegranate seeds for dried and chop up fresh strawberries for an easy spin on this cocktail. Can't find dried basil? Muddle fresh basil in the shaker before adding the tea!

The Tea-quila Popper may be taken as a shot, or—if you really want it to "pop"—lightly slammed onto a table with one hand covering the shot glass, and then quickly thrown back.

TEA-QUILA POPPER

This is the cocktail for ladies' night. We've heard tequila is a truth serum . . . so gossip away!

TEA BASE
½ teaspoon dried lemon verbena

½ teaspoon ground ginger

Pinch of dried peppermint

COCKTAIL
1 oz brewed tea base

1 oz tequila

½ tablespoon agave nectar

Splash of Champagne

Makes 1 cocktail

In a cup, place 3 oz of room temperature water. You will only use 1 oz for the tea base in this recipe, so don't worry if there is extra left over. Feel free to sip, save, or discard!

In a tea linen or tea ball, combine all of the ingredients for the tea base. Brew in the room temperature water for 10 minutes, agitating from time to time. Remove the sachet/ball.

In a shaker, combine 1 oz of the tea base, the tequila, and agave nectar. Dry-shake until the agave dissolves. Add ice and gently swirl to chill. Strain and pour into a glass. Top with the Champagne.

GREEN PEACH

This gingery pick-me-up is chock-full of vitamin C and antioxidants—and, bonus, it's also an energy-booster.

TEA BASE
¾ teaspoon green tea leaves

¾ teaspoon dried peach

½ teaspoon ground ginger

COCKTAIL
4½ oz brewed tea base

1½ oz mezcal

1 tablespoon agave nectar

GARNISH
Candied ginger

Makes 1 cocktail

In a cup, place 6 oz of room temperature water. You will only use 4½ oz for the tea base in this recipe, so don't worry if there is extra left over. Feel free to sip, save, or discard!

In a tea linen or tea ball, combine all of the ingredients for the tea base. Brew in the room temperature water for 10 minutes, agitating from time to time. Remove the sachet/ball.

In a shaker, combine 4½ oz of the tea base, the mezcal, and the agave nectar. Dry-shake until the agave dissolves. Pour into a glass over ice and gently swirl to chill. Garnish with candied ginger.

Feeling extra gingery? Try pairing our Green Peach cocktail with the Ginger Tea Sweet Potato Soup. Perfectly spiced and delicious!

Ginger Tea Sweet Potato Soup

contributed by Chris Mitchell, Bubby's

///////////// /// /// / /// /// ////////////

3 tablespoons ginger tea leaves

1 tablespoon canola oil

2 large yellow onions, diced

1-inch piece fresh ginger, peeled

1 teaspoon toasted cumin seeds

1 teaspoon toasted coriander seeds

1 teaspoon toasted Szechuan peppercorns

4 large sweet potatoes, cut into 1-inch pieces

1 quart heavy cream

1 tablespoon Worcestershire sauce

1 tablespoon sriracha sauce

Salt

Lime zest and juice

Serves 6

Boil 3 quarts of water and pour it over the ginger tea in a heat-safe bowl. Let steep for 6 to 8 minutes.

Heat the oil in a stockpot over medium heat. Add the onions and cook for about 10 minutes, until translucent. Add the ginger, cumin, coriander, and peppercorns and cook for another 3 minutes. Add the sweet potatoes and stir to coat for 3 minutes. Add the tea and cream and bring to a boil. Turn the heat down to a simmer and add the Worcestershire and sriracha. Let simmer for another 30 minutes, until the sweet potatoes are fork-tender.

In the pot, use a hand blender to pulse the soup to a velvety smooth consistency (or do this in small batches in a conventional blender). When the mixture is completely smooth, add it back to the pot and simmer again for 15 minutes, until ready to serve. Finish with lime zest and juice.

CINCO DE MAYO

The name gives it away—this was made for the fifth of May!

TEA BASE
½ teaspoon green tea leaves

½ teaspoon yerba maté

½ teaspoon dried peach

½ teaspoon ground ginger

COCKTAIL
4½ oz brewed tea base

1½ oz tequila

1 tablespoon agave nectar

GARNISH
1 fresh ginger slice

Makes 1 cocktail

In a cup, place 6 oz of room temperature water. You will use 4½ oz for the tea base in this recipe, so don't worry if there is extra left over. Feel free to sip, save, or discard!

In a tea linen or tea ball, combine all of the ingredients for the tea base. Brew in the room temperature water for 10 minutes, agitating from time to time. Remove the sachet/ball.

In a shaker, combine 4½ oz of the tea base, the tequila, and the agave nectar. Dry-shake until the agave dissolves. Add ice to the shaker and gently swirl to chill. Garnish with the ginger slice. Strain and pour into a glass.

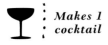

Can't find dried peach? Use fresh instead!

RED MARIA

Our version of the Bloody Mary includes energizing Assam . . . a perfect hangover-busting addition.

TEA BASE
2 teaspoons Assam tea leaves

COCKTAIL
4 oz brewed tea base

16 oz Clamato juice

4 oz tequila

4 oz red wine

5 dashes of Worcestershire sauce

4 dashes of hot sauce

2 pinches of celery salt

2 pinches of salt

2 pinches of black pepper

GARNISH
Castelvetrano olives

Lime wedges

In a cup, place 6 oz of room temperature water. You will use 4 oz for the tea base in this recipe, so don't worry if there is extra left over. Feel free to sip, save, or discard!

Fill a tea linen or tea ball with the Assam tea. Brew in the room temperature water for 10 minutes, agitating from time to time. Remove the sachet/ball.

In a large pitcher, combine the Clamato juice, tequila, wine, Worcestershire sauce, hot sauce, celery salt, salt, and pepper. Add 4 oz of the tea base. Gently swirl.

Add more spice, to taste. Serve over ice. Garnish with the olives and lime wedges.

*Makes
28 oz*

WHITE + BLUE

Subtle and refreshing, the White + Blue can be sipped anytime of the year! Stimulating to both the body and mind, this blend is high in vitamins C and K, which help clear the body of toxins.

• •

TEA BASE
1 teaspoon Assam tea leaves

¼ teaspoon chopped vanilla bean

¾ teaspoon dried blueberries

Pinch of blueberry leaf (optional)

COCKTAIL
3 oz brewed tea base

3 oz white wine

1 oz elderflower liqueur

GARNISH
Fresh blueberries

Makes 1 cocktail

In a cup, place 5 oz of room temperature water. You will use only 3 oz for the tea base in this recipe, so don't worry if there is extra left over. Feel free to sip, save, or discard!

In a tea linen or tea ball, combine all of the ingredients for the tea base. Brew in the room temperature water for 10 minutes, agitating from time to time. Remove the sachet/ball.

In a shaker, combine 3 oz of the tea base, the wine, and elderflower liqueur. Dry-shake to combine. Add ice and gently swirl to chill. Strain and pour into a glass or serve with ice. Float fresh blueberries on top.

WHITE HORSE WINE

This tea-based sangria is a crowd favorite. Loaded with antioxidants and vitamin C, the White Horse is the perfect balance of naughty and nice.

TEA BASE
½ teaspoon white tea leaves

½ teaspoon chopped lemongrass

¾ teaspoon dried peach

¼ teaspoon dried lemon peel

COCKTAIL
12 oz brewed tea base

12 oz white wine

¼ cup agave nectar

GARNISH
Fresh peach slices and blueberries

Makes 24 oz

In a cup, place 13 oz of room temperature water. You will only use 12 oz for the tea base in this recipe, so don't worry if there is extra left over. Feel free to sip, save, or discard!

You will need to use two tea linens or tea balls for this base. Evenly distribute the tea base ingredients into the two linens. Tie off the tea linens (or close the tea balls) and place them in the room temperature water. Brew for 10 minutes, agitating from time to time. Remove the sachets/balls.

In a large pitcher, combine 12 oz of the tea base, the wine, and agave nectar. Stir until the agave dissolves. Float in the fresh peach slices and blueberries. Chill for at least 1 hour before serving or pour over ice and serve immediately.

PUNCH EAST

This was first served in East Hampton at a polo match where Nic Roldan led a team against Nacho Figueras. We were sipping pretty!

TEA BASE
Mix together in equal parts and use 1 full teaspoon:
Dried peach

Dried apricot

Dried orange peel

Cloves

Cinnamon

Black pepper

COCKTAIL
4 oz brewed tea base

1 oz pineapple juice

1 tablespoon agave nectar

4 oz sparkling white wine

GARNISH
1 orange twist

In a cup, place 6 oz of room temperature water. You will only use 4 oz for the tea base in this recipe, so don't worry if there is extra left over. Feel free to sip, save, or discard!

In a tea linen or tea ball, combine all of the ingredients for the tea base. Brew in the room temperature water for 10 minutes, agitating from time to time. Remove the sachet/ball.

In a shaker, combine 4 oz of the tea base, the pineapple juice, and agave nectar. Dry-shake until the agave dissolves. Add ice to the shaker and gently swirl to chill. Strain and pour into a glass. Top with the sparkling wine and swirl gently again. Garnish with the orange twist.

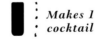

Makes 1 cocktail

SSSSPICY

Hot or cold, this cleansing and invigorating cocktail will awaken all of your senses.

• • • • • ' ' ' ' ' ' ' ' ' • ' ' ' • • • • • • • • - -

TEA BASE
Mix together in equal parts and use 2 teaspoons:
Dried jasmine flowers

Rose petals

Chopped cinnamon stick

Dried cardamom

Dried cloves

Dried ginger

COCKTAIL
4½ oz brewed tea base

1½ oz spiced rum

½ tablespoon agave nectar

GARNISH
1 cinnamon stick (hot) or ground cinnamon (cold)

To serve hot: Heat 5 oz of water until hot (but not boiling) and pour into a heat-safe mug. In a tea linen or tea ball, combine all of the ingredients for the tea base. Brew in the hot water for 5 minutes, gently agitating from time to time. Remove the sachet/ball.

Add the rum and agave nectar and stir until the agave dissolves. Pour into a heat-safe mug and garnish with the cinnamon stick.

To serve cold: In a cup, place 6 oz of room temperature water. You will only use 4½ oz for the tea base in this recipe, so don't worry if there is extra left over. Feel free to sip, save, or discard! In a tea linen or tea ball, combine all of the ingredients for the tea base. Brew in the room temperature

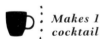
Makes 1 cocktail

water for 10 minutes, agitating from time to time. Remove the sachet/ball.

In a shaker, combine 4½ oz of the tea base, the rum, and agave nectar. Dry-shake until the agave dissolves. Pour into a glass over ice. Swirl gently to chill. Sprinkle ground cinnamon on top.

VANILLA BEACH

For the sweet days of summer, this blend is loaded with electrolytes. It's hydrating and chock-full of antioxidants and vitamin C.

TEA BASE

¼ teaspoon chopped vanilla bean

¾ teaspoon rooibos

½ teaspoon dried blueberries

½ teaspoon dried strawberries

COCKTAIL

4½ oz brewed tea base

1½ oz spiced rum

1 tablespoon agave nectar

Makes 1 cocktail

In a cup, place 6 oz of room temperature water. You will use 4½ oz for the tea base in this recipe, so don't worry if there is extra left over. Feel free to sip, save, or discard!

In a tea linen or tea ball, combine all of the ingredients for the tea base. Brew in the room temperature water for 10 minutes, agitating from time to time. Remove the sachet/ball.

In a shaker, combine 4½ oz of the tea base, the rum, and the agave nectar. Dry-shake until the agave dissolves. Pour into a glass over ice and swirl gently to chill.

We were invited to the Captain Morgan headquarters to serve up a couple of treats for their team . . . and Vanilla Beach was a hit!

BLACK + PINK

This good-for-you blend contains cleansing hibiscus and energy-boosting Darjeeling tea.

TEA BASE
1¼ teaspoons Darjeeling tea leaves

¾ teaspoon dried hibiscus flowers

COCKTAIL
4½ oz brewed tea base

1½ oz gin

1 tablespoon agave nectar

GARNISH
1 fresh strawberry

Makes 1 cocktail

In a cup, place 6 oz of room temperature water. You will only use 4½ oz for the tea base in this recipe, so don't worry if there is extra left over. Feel free to sip, save, or discard!

In a tea linen or tea ball, combine the Darjeeling tea and hibiscus flowers. Brew in the room temperature water for 10 minutes, agitating from time to time. Remove the sachet/ball.

In a shaker, combine 4½ oz of the tea base, the gin, and agave nectar. Dry-shake until the agave dissolves. Pour into a glass over ice and gently swirl to chill. Garnish with the strawberry.

THE BEST PART ABOUT BREWIN' IT UP FOR TEA COCKTAILS? You can double-dip toward your health. Brew a big batch and you'll be able to enjoy your cocktails, and then sip on mood- and metabolism-boosting iced tea all week! It will stay good in your fridge for up to 5 days.

UNDERGROUND CHAI

This blend is full of antioxidants, is great for the digestive and respiratory systems, and has antibacterial and anti-inflammatory properties.

TEA BASE

2 teaspoons black Masala chai

Pinch of dried jasmine flowers

COCKTAIL

3½ oz brewed tea base

2 oz white wine

1 oz sloe gin

½ oz elderflower liqueur

½ tablespoon agave nectar

2 oz soda water

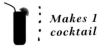

Makes 1 cocktail

In a cup, place 6 oz of room temperature water. You will only use 3½ oz for the tea base in this recipe, so don't worry if there is extra left over. Feel free to sip, save, or discard!

In a tea linen or tea ball, combine the black Masala chai and jasmine flowers. Brew in the room temperature water for 10 minutes, agitating from time to time. Remove the sachet/ball.

In a shaker, combine 3½ oz of the tea base, the wine, sloe gin, elderflower liqueur, and agave nectar. Dry-shake until the agave dissolves. Pour into a glass over ice. Top with the soda water and gently swirl.

FOR WHOM THE BELL FLOWER TOLLS

contributed by Lynnette Marrero, mixologist ←

A floral treat from a great bartender.

• • • • , ' ' ' ' ' ' ' ' ' • ' ' ' ' ' ' ' ' ' ' ' ' ' ' ' ' '

TEA BASE
½ teaspoon green rooibos

⅓ teaspoon dried hibiscus flowers

¼ teaspoon dried lemon peel

¼ teaspoon dried raspberries

COCKTAIL
1 oz brewed tea base

1¼ oz American Fruits sour cherry liqueur

¾ oz Tanqueray gin

¼ oz lemon juice

1 teaspoon Lemon Oleo*

Dash of Angostura bitters

Sparkling water

GARNISH
Cinnamon stick or star anise pod

In a cup, place 3 oz of room temperature water. You will only use 1 oz for the tea base in this recipe, so don't worry if there is extra left over. Feel free to sip, save, or discard!

In a tea linen or tea ball, combine all of the ingredients for the tea base. Brew in the room temperature water for 10 minutes, agitating from time to time. Remove the sachet/ball.

In a shaker, combine 1 oz of the tea base, sour cherry liqueur, gin, lemon juice, Lemon Oleo, and bitters. Dry-shake to combine. Top with sparkling water. Pour into a glass and garnish with the cinnamon or star anise.

Makes 1 cocktail

*First, zest a few lemons, leaving behind most of the white pith. Place in a bowl, add 2 oz sugar for each lemon's worth of peel, and stir to combine. Let rest for an hour or longer. Strain the liquid that has pooled in the bowl, and discard the solids.

THE EARL

The tea base is rich in vitamin C and is excellent for the entire system.

TEA BASE

¾ teaspoon Earl Grey tea leaves

¾ teaspoon dried lemon verbena

¼ teaspoon dried jasmine flowers

¼ teaspoon dried peppermint

Pinch of dried lemon peel

COCKTAIL

3½ oz brewed tea base

1½ oz gin

1 tablespoon agave nectar

2 oz soda water

Juice from 1 lemon wedge

In a cup, place 6 oz of room temperature water. You will only use 3½ oz for the tea base in this recipe, so don't worry if there is extra left over. Feel free to sip, save, or discard!

In a tea linen or tea ball, combine all of the ingredients for the tea base. Brew in the room temperature water for 10 minutes, agitating from time to time. Remove the sachet/ball.

In a shaker, combine 3½ oz of the tea base, the gin, and agave nectar. Dry-shake until the agave dissolves. Pour into a glass over ice and swirl gently to chill. Top with the soda water and squeeze in the juice from the lemon wedge.

Makes 1 cocktail

UPPER EAST SIDER

The Upper East Sider refreshes the senses.

• • • • • , ' , • , • , • , • . • , • • • • • • • • • • • • • •

TEA BASE
1 teaspoon dried lemon verbena

1 teaspoon dried peppermint

COCKTAIL
3½ oz brewed tea base

1½ oz whiskey

1 tablespoon simple syrup

1 lemon wedge

2 oz soda water

GARNISH
1 sprig fresh mint

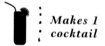

Makes 1 cocktail

In a cup, place 6 oz of room temperature water. You will use 3½ oz for the tea base in this recipe, so don't worry if there is extra left over. Feel free to sip, save, or discard!

In a tea linen or tea ball, combine the lemon verbena and peppermint. Brew in the room temperature water for 10 minutes, agitating from time to time. Remove the sachet/ball.

In a shaker, combine 3½ oz of the tea base, the whiskey, and the simple syrup, and squeeze in the lemon wedge. Dry-shake to combine. Pour into a glass over ice and gently swirl to chill. Top with soda water and gently stir again. Garnish with the mint sprig.

Originally created and served at the after-party for the *Sex and the City* movie premiere!

SWEET NOTHINGS TODDY

Perfect for nighttime sipping, rooibos has natural electrolytes and contains no caffeine.

TEA BASE
1¼ teaspoons rooibos

½ teaspoon chopped vanilla bean

¼ teaspoon black pepper

COCKTAIL
3 oz brewed tea base

3 oz milk

1½ oz bourbon

1 tablespoon sugar

GARNISH
1 cinnamon stick and ground cinnamon

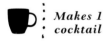 *Makes 1 cocktail*

Heat 6 oz of water until hot (but not boiling) and pour into a heat-safe container. You will use only 3 oz for the tea base in this recipe, so don't worry if there is extra left over. Feel free to sip, save, or discard!

In a tea linen or tea ball, combine all of the ingredients for the tea base. Brew in the hot water for 5 minutes, gently agitating from time to time. Remove the tea sachet/ball.

Pour 3 oz of the tea base into a saucepan. Add the milk, bourbon, and sugar. Let sit over low heat, stirring from time to time, for 5 minutes, or until the sugar dissolves.

Pour into a heat-safe mug and garnish with the cinnamon stick and ground cinnamon.

NO BIGGER THAN A NEEDLE'S EYE

contributed by Warren Bobrow, cocktail whisperer/ barman

For all our thirsty friends.

GREEN MINT TEA
4 teaspoons green tea leaves

½ cup fresh mint leaves, carefully washed and dried

Honey (about 2 tablespoons)

RHUBARB TEA
2 tablespoons rhubarb, diced

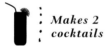

Makes 2 cocktails

The day before: Heat 5 oz of water until hot (but not boiling) and pour into a heat-safe bowl. Fill a tea linen or tea ball with the green tea leaves. Brew in the hot water for 4 minutes, gently agitating from time to time. Remove the sachet/ball. Add the mint leaves to the tea. Steep the mint in the green tea overnight in a cool place.

The next day: Strain out the mint and sweeten the tea, to taste, with honey.

Heat 5 oz of water until hot (but not boiling) and pour into a heat-safe mug. Add rhubarb. Brew in the hot water for 4 minutes, gently agitating from time to time. Strain out the rhubarb.

COCKTAIL
1½ oz Templeton rye

1 oz rhubarb tea

4 oz brewed
green mint tea

A splash of seltzer

4 drops Bitter Truth
orange bitters

GARNISH
Fresh mint leaves

Fill two glasses with 2-inch ice cubes or hand-cut ice if you have the time. Divide the rye and rhubarb tea between the glasses. Top equally with the mint tea and finish with the seltzer—just a splash! Drip the bitters over the top. Garnish with the mint leaves.

We Love Water

BREWING TEAS FOR SO LONG HAS LEFT US WITH A PRETTY bizarre sixth sense regarding water—we can suss out wherever the nearest faucet is and immediately take note of knobs, water pressure, sink depth, and more. It's not a very useful skill now, but we just can't kick the habit!

And we'll never forget about the time we were brewing for a super-swanky private party . . . and the sink was automatic. You'd never think about the ramifications of this when holding your hands underneath to wash them, but filling up a number of pitchers of water?? Not so easy! Maria practically got carpal tunnel syndrome swiping her hand in front the sensor all night long, and Jennie was near tears. But there ya have it, an unlikely sixth sense!

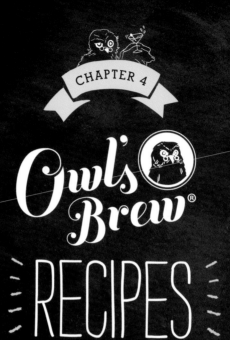

CHAPTER 4

Owl's Brew®

RECIPES

Owl's Brew is the first-ever tea-based cocktail mixer. We've brewed up and bottled our favorite loose-leaf blends, packaged them in a chic and handsome way (or so we think!), and now they are ready for you to pour at home!

THREE BLENDS

Below is an overview of our three original blends and their flavor profiles. Check out our Web site for new blends and seasonal specials at theowlsbrew.com.

THE CLASSIC
English Breakfast tea with lemon and lime—"English Breakfast with a Tart Twist"

PINK & BLACK
Darjeeling tea with hibiscus, strawberry, and lemon—"Darjeeling with a Hint of Hibiscus"

COCO-LADA
Black tea with chai spices, coconut, and pineapple—"Sweet with a Spicy Kick"

Create the following cocktails with our special Owl's Brew blends. We raise a glass to the at-home entertainers and hope these recipes up your cocktail game.

BLACK AMBER

A whiskey cocktail for beer lovers.

2 oz Owl's Brew
Pink & Black

1 oz whiskey

2 oz pomegranate
juice

6 oz amber ale
(chilled)

In a shaker, combine the Pink &
Black, whiskey, and pomegranate
juice. Shake with ice. Strain and
pour into a glass. Top with the ale
and gently swirl.

*Makes 1
cocktail*

WAKE ME WHEN IT'S OVER

contributed by
Chris Mitchell,
Bubby's

The perfect nightcap.

1 oz Owl's Brew
Pink & Black

2 oz rye

1 oz grapefruit juice

Dash of grapefruit
bitters

In a shaker, combine the Pink &
Black, rye, grapefruit juice, and
bitters. Shake with ice. Strain and
pour into a glass.

*Makes 1
cocktail*

Black Amber

Red Whiskey

RED WHISKEY

Earthy and delightful!

2 oz Owl's Brew
The Classic

2 oz fresh-pressed
beet juice

1½ oz whiskey

1 lemon slice,
for garnish

In a shaker, combine The Classic, beet juice, and whiskey. Shake with ice and pour into a glass. Garnish with the lemon slice.

 *Makes 1 cocktail*

THE NEW YORKER

Manhattan with a citrus twist.

3 oz Owl's Brew
Pink & Black

1½ oz bourbon

Dash of orange
bitters

1 orange or lemon
twist, for garnish

Makes 1 cocktail

In a shaker, combine the Pink & Black, bourbon, and bitters. Shake with ice. Strain and pour into a glass. Garnish with the orange or lemon twist.

>>> The perfect cocktail for those suspicious of drinking tea after dark. A dear uncle was a major holdout on tea cocktails until giving this one a whirl.

THE BOURBON BUBBLER

An effervescent tipple.

contributed by Chris
Mitchell, Bubby's

**4 oz Owl's Brew
Pink & Black**

2 oz bourbon

3 oz sparkling water

**Fresh strawberries,
for garnish**

In a shaker with ice combine the
Pink & Black and bourbon. Pour
into a glass over ice. Top with
sparkling water and garnish with
fresh strawberries.

*Makes 1
cocktail*

OWL'S TODDY

Our perfectly spiced winter warmer!

**3 oz Owl's Brew
The Classic**

1½ oz bourbon

3 apple slices

**1 cinnamon stick,
for garnish**

In a saucepan, combine The Classic,
bourbon, and apple slices. Simmer
over low heat for 8 minutes. Do not
boil. Remove from the heat and pour
into a heat-safe mug. Garnish with
the cinnamon stick.

*Makes 1
cocktail*

We served this when we
checked out Summit Series in
the winter of 2013. It was the
perfect mountaintop sipper.

We first met Chris Mitchell when we launched our Owl's Hour program at his pop-up location in NYC's Meatpacking District in the summer of 2013. We're obsessed with his delicious cocktails (and food recipes)!

The Bourbon Bubbler

OWL'S NOG

A coconut twist for a classic nog.

• • • • ✓ • • • ✓ • ✓ • • • • • • • • • • • • • • • •

2 oz Owl's Brew Coco-Lada

2 oz eggnog

1½ oz bourbon

1 cinnamon stick and ground cinnamon, for garnish

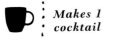 *Makes 1 cocktail*

To serve hot: In a saucepan, combine the Coco-Lada, eggnog, and bourbon. Simmer over low heat for 8 minutes. Do not boil. Remove from the heat and pour into a heat-safe mug. Garnish with the cinnamon stick and a sprinkle of ground cinnamon.

To serve chilled: In a shaker, combine the Coco-Lada, eggnog, and bourbon. Shake with ice and pour into a glass. Sprinkle with ground cinnamon.

JENNIE'S GARDEN

For the love of green.

contributed by Chris Mitchell, Bubby's

2 oz Owl's Brew
The Classic

2 oz fresh-pressed
cucumber juice

1½ oz gin

1 fresh mint leaf,
for garnish

In a shaker, combine The Classic, cucumber juice, and gin. Shake with ice. Strain and pour into a glass. Garnish with the mint leaf.

 Makes 1 cocktail

THE GIN PANTHER

The perfect gin cocktail.

3 oz Owl's Brew
Pink & Black

1½ oz gin

1 lime slice,
for garnish

In a shaker, combine the Pink & Black and gin. Shake with ice and pour into a glass. Garnish with the lime slice.

 Makes 1 cocktail

True story: At the age of four, Jennie had a garden that her grandfather called Jennie's Garden—it was a mini version of her Popop's garden. They both grew cucumbers.

Jennie's Garden

HERB OWL

For the botanist in you.

. . . .

2 fresh sprigs dill, for muddle and garnish

3 oz Owl's Brew The Classic

1½ oz gin

½ oz lemon juice

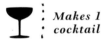

Makes 1 cocktail

In a shaker, muddle the dill. Add The Classic, gin, and lemon juice. Shake with ice. Strain and pour into a glass. Garnish with a dill sprig.

A good friend of Jennie's asked her to come up with the perfect cocktail for a late-June picnic. The Herb Owl was born!

SWEET PUP

A salty sunrise.

- -

1½ oz Owl's Brew Pink & Black

1½ oz cranberry juice

1½ oz gin

¼ teaspoon salt

In a shaker, combine the Pink & Black, cranberry juice, gin, and salt. Shake with ice. Strain and pour into a glass.

 *Makes 1 cocktail*

THE BASIL BERRY

A little earthy gem.

- -

5 fresh basil leaves, for muddle and garnish

Fresh raspberries

3 oz Owl's Brew The Classic

1½ oz gin

In a shaker, muddle the basil leaves and raspberries. Add The Classic and gin. Shake with ice. Pour into a glass. Garnish with a basil leaf.

 Makes 1 cocktail

We didn't originally have salt in this one—we were sitting by a pool and a buddy of ours, who is also a chef, improvised. We loved it so much, we changed the recipe!

Sweet Pup

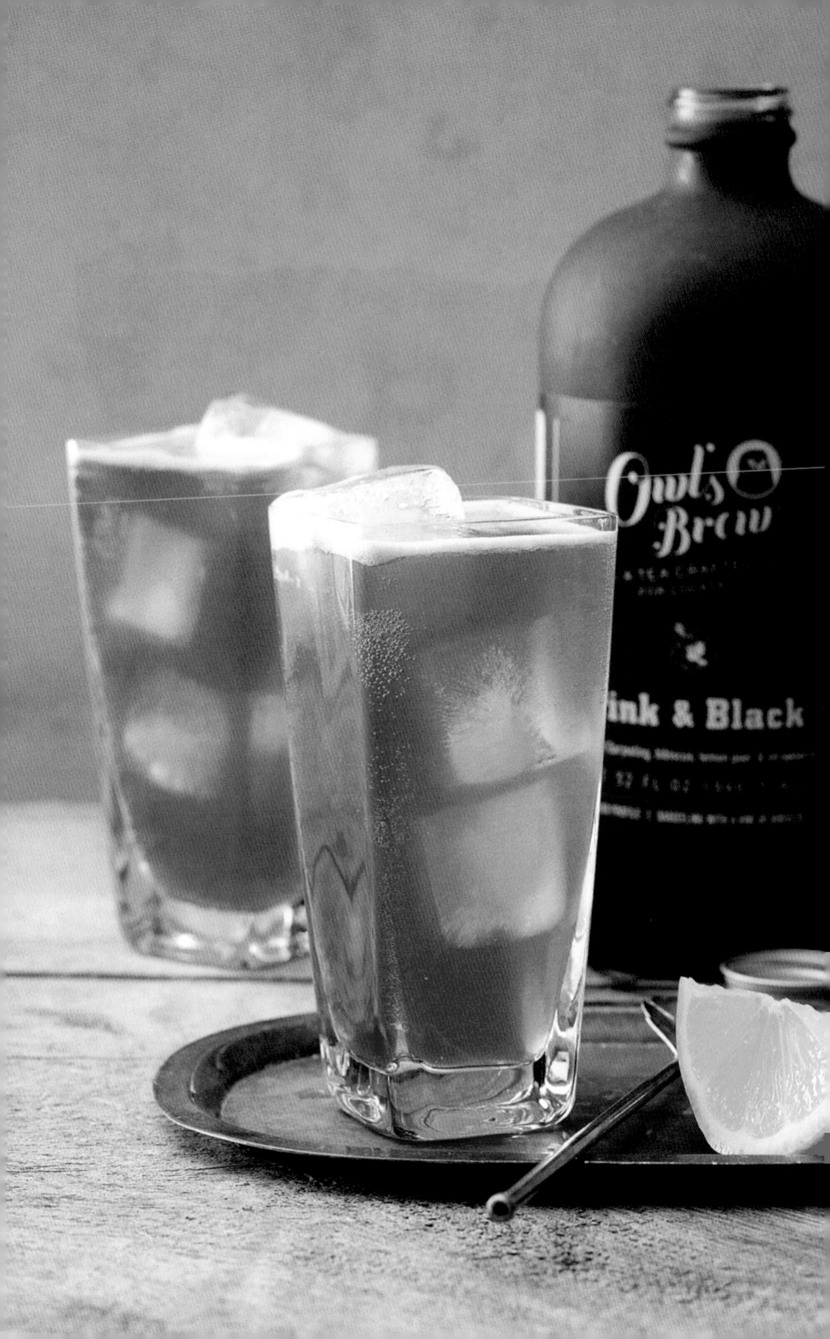
Owl's Brew
ink & Black

17TH HOUR

← contributed by Walter Easterbrook, mixologist

A sparkling botanical.

4 oz Owl's Brew Pink & Black

1½ oz The Botanist gin

¼ oz lemon juice

Splash of Q Club club soda

In a shaker, combine the Pink & Black, gin, and lemon juice. Shake with ice and pour into a glass. Top with club soda.

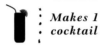

Makes 1 cocktail

This cocktail was first served at the Bowery Hotel in NYC!

OWL-EYED

Tart watermelon.

contributed by Chris Mitchell, Bubby's

2 oz Owl's Brew The Classic

3 oz gin

2 oz fresh-pressed watermelon juice

In a shaker, combine The Classic, gin, and watermelon juice. Shake with ice. Strain and pour into a glass.

Makes 1 cocktail

We tried to create a signature look called Owl Eye in which we made a monocle with our fingers. We encountered a road bump when we realized that Maria cannot extend her arm in the air and then bend her elbow in order to center a monocle around her eye. Chris created this cocktail for us before we had this devastating knowledge.

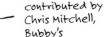

THE RIGHT SWIPE ←

contributed by
Chris Mitchell,
Bubby's

Yes, this is a Tinder reference. Cringe.

. . . .

FRESNO CHILE-INFUSED AÑEJO RUM*
½ Fresno chile

3 oz añejo rum

CILANTRO SIMPLE SYRUP
¼ cup sugar

¼ cup water

1 fresh sprig cilantro

COCKTAIL
3 oz Owl's Brew Pink & Black

1 oz lime juice

1 oz cilantro simple syrup

3 oz Fresno chile–infused añejo rum

Add the chile to the rum. We recommend leaving the rum to infuse for 24 hours for the fullest flavor. The longer the chile sits, the spicier the cocktail will be.

In a small saucepan, combine the sugar, water, and cilantro and bring to a boil. Simmer until the sugar is dissolved, about 3 minutes. Remove from the heat and let cool. (You will have more simple syrup than you need for a single cocktail.)

In a shaker, combine the Pink & Black, lime juice, cilantro simple syrup, and rum. Shake with ice and pour into a glass.

To infuse an entire bottle of rum (750ml), use 4 Fresno chiles, piercing them to expose the interior.

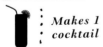 *Makes 1 cocktail*

OWL THYME

With an herbaceous bite.

• • • • ⁄ ⁄ • ⁄ • ⁄ • • ⁄ • • ⁄ • • • • • • • • • •

**3 oz Owl's Brew
The Classic**

1½ oz white rum

**2 fresh sprigs
thyme, for muddle
and garnish**

In a shaker, combine The Classic, rum, and thyme. Muddle the thyme, then shake with ice and pour into a glass. Garnish with a thyme sprig.

*Makes 1
cocktail*

CHA-CHA-CHAI

Not your grandma's chai.

• • • • ⁄ ⁄ • ⁄ • ⁄ • • ⁄ • • ⁄ • • • • • • • • • •

**3 oz Owl's Brew
Coco-Lada**

1½ oz spiced rum

**2 cinnamon sticks,
for garnish**

In a saucepan, combine the Coco-Lada, rum, and cinnamon sticks. Simmer over low heat for 8 minutes. Remove from the heat and pour into a heat-safe mug. Garnish with the cinnamon sticks.

*Makes 1
cocktail*

Owl Thyme

Sure Thing

SURE THING ← *contributed by Kevin Denton, mixologist*

For the brave and the bold.

• •

2 oz aged rhum agricole*

½ oz Fernet-Vallet

½ oz barley malt syrup

Owl's Brew Coco-Lada foam

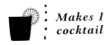

Makes 1 cocktail

In a shaker, combine the rhum agricole, Fernet-Vallet, and barley malt syrup. Shake with ice. Strain and pour into a rocks glass. Top with the foam.

To make the foam: Add 4 oz of Owl's Brew Coco-Lada and 1 egg white to an iSi whipper. Charge with two nitrous oxide canisters and shake vigorously. After 4 minutes, it will be ready to use.

*Kevin recommends Rhum Clément aged barrel select.

PIRATE'S BOOTY ← *contributed by Chris Mitchell, Bubby's*

A true boat drink.

• •

1½ oz spiced rum

1 oz Owl's Brew Coco-Lada

¾ oz pineapple juice

2 dashes of orange bitters

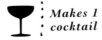

Makes 1 cocktail

In a shaker, combine the rum, Coco-Lada, pineapple juice, and bitters. Shake with ice. Strain and pour into a glass.

OWL'S PIÑA

File this one under "staycation sipper."

• • • • • ' • • • ' • ' ' • • ' • ' • • • • • • • • • • • •

3 oz Owl's Brew Coco-Lada

1½ oz spiced rum

Pineapple wedge, for garnish

In a shaker, combine the Coco-Lada and rum. Shake with ice and pour into a glass. Garnish with the pineapple wedge.

Makes 1 cocktail

Hosting a Party?

TRY THE OWL'S PIÑA IN A PUNCH BOWL! THIS SUMMERY cocktail is always a hit. The pour is 2 parts Owl's Brew Coco-Lada to 1 part spiced rum—as long as you double the ratio of Owl's Brew to liquor in the bowl, it will be delicious! Try floating fresh pineapple slices in the punch bowl, or, if you're feeling festive, serve it up in a coconut.

A good friend of Jennie's hosted a Staycation party one cold NYC winter. We dreamed up this piña colada–like cocktail in honor of the big event.

Rise & Shine

RISE & SHINE

A morning libation.

• • • • • ◦ ◦ ◦ ◦ ◦ • ◦ ◦ • ◦ ◦ • • ◦ • • • • • • • • • •

1½ oz vodka

½ oz Owl's Brew
Pink & Black

½ oz sweet
vermouth

1 oz orange juice

1½ oz cranberry
juice

In a shaker, combine the vodka, Pink & Black, vermouth, orange juice, and cranberry juice. Shake with ice and pour into a glass.

 Makes 1 cocktail

DARK + BREW

Gingery and bold.

• • • • • ◦ ◦ ◦ ◦ ◦ • ◦ ◦ • ◦ ◦ • • ◦ • • • • • • • • • •

2 oz Owl's Brew
Coco-Lada

1½ oz vodka

½ oz ginger liqueur

2 oz ginger beer

1 lime wedge,
for garnish

In a shaker, combine the Coco-Lada, vodka, and ginger liqueur. Shake with ice and pour into a glass. Top with the ginger beer and garnish with the lime.

 Makes 1 cocktail

THE MARCIANO PUNCH

contributed by Bryan Schneider, bar director, Park Avenue

Brunching perfection.

• •

2 oz vodka

1 oz Owl's Brew The Classic

¾ oz lemon juice

½ oz honey

1 lemon slice and fresh raspberries, for garnish

In a shaker, combine the vodka, The Classic, lemon juice, and honey. Dry-shake until the honey dissolves. Pour into a glass over ice. Garnish with the lemon slice and raspberries.

Makes 1 cocktail

THE MASTER CLEANSE

Retox your detox.

• •

1 fresh ginger slice

3 oz Owl's Brew The Classic

1½ oz vodka

Pinch of cayenne pepper

In a shaker, muddle the ginger. Add The Classic and vodka. Sprinkle with cayenne pepper, as you like. Shake with ice. Strain and pour into a glass.

Makes 1 cocktail

Cocktails with a Kick

SHAKE, STIR, OR SPRINKLE YOUR WAY TO A COCKTAIL WITH A KICK.
Here's our easy cheat sheet to upping your cocktail game in a
"pinch"!

Use dried or fresh chile peppers. If you simply want a little heat,
remove the seeds from the peppers—or leave them in if you are looking for a fire!

~~~~~~~~~~~~~~~~~~~~~~~~~~~~~~

HABAÑERO CHILE
Habañeros are one of the
hottest peppers available in the
United States. They are floral
and tangy. Try adding them to
cocktails with a tropical fruit or a
tomato base.

JALAPEÑO CHILE
These peppers are very common
in cocktails and are moderately
spicy. They have a sweet flavor,
similar to a spicy bell pepper. Try
adding some jalapeños to
cocktails with a herbaceous,
fruity, or tart base.

CHIPOTLE CHILE
These ripe, dried jalapeños offer
a smoky finish and pair well with
fruity, citrusy cocktails.

ANCHO CHILE
These peppers have moderate
heat, with a mild, fruity flavor
and earthy notes. They are
delicious when added to cocktails
with a tart base or when paired
with mezcal or tequila.

CAYENNE CHILE
This hot pepper packs a punch.
It's most commonly available
ground in a jar, but you can also
find fresh peppers. With a fiery
and floral flavor profile, it works
perfectly with citrusy or
herbaceous cocktails.

THE GREEN GARDEN

Leafy goodness.

3 oz Owl's Brew The Classic

3 oz fresh-pressed green juice*

1 oz vodka

1 oz sake

1 lemon slice, for garnish

Makes 1 cocktail

In a shaker, combine The Classic, green juice, vodka, and sake. Shake with ice and pour into a mason jar. Garnish with the lemon wedge.

*We recommend a green juice with mixed greens with apple and lemon wedges.

We debuted this cocktail at an OK! magazine happy hour in Los Angeles.

AUTUMN LEAVES ← contributed by Josh Curtis, mixologist

A gingery treat.

• •

TEA BASE
1 teaspoon oolong
tea leaves

COCKTAIL
1 oz brewed tea base

1½ oz Akvinta vodka

1 oz Owl's Brew
Coco-Lada

¾ oz lemon juice

½ oz fresh-pressed
ginger juice

1 fresh sage leaf

*Makes 1
cocktail*

Fill a cup with 4 oz of room temperature water. Fill your tea linen or tea ball with the oolong tea leaves. Place the linen in the water and let brew for 10 minutes.

After 10 minutes, remove the tea linen, and measure 1 oz of brewed tea. Pour the tea into the shaker and add the vodka, Coco-Lada, lemon juice, and ginger juice. Dry-shake.

Pour into a glass over ice. Garnish with the sage.

EISBAR ← contributed by Gates Otsuji, The Standard Hotel

Citrusy and full-bodied.

2 oz vodka

1 oz Owl's Brew Coco-Lada

½ oz lemon juice

¼ oz Becherovka

¼ oz simple syrup

1 piece orange peel, for garnish

In a shaker, combine the vodka, Coco-Lada, lemon juice, Becherovka, and simple syrup. Shake with ice. Strain and pour into a glass. Garnish with the orange peel.

Makes 1 cocktail

THE ELDER

A floral classic.

3 oz Owl's Brew The Classic

1½ oz vodka

½ oz elderflower liqueur

1 piece lemon peel, for garnish

In a shaker, combine The Classic, vodka, and elderflower liqueur. Shake with ice and pour into a glass. Garnish with the lemon peel.

Makes 1 cocktail

IMPEACHED

Sweet and smoky southern tea time.

• • • • • ′ ′ ′ • ′ • • ′ • • ′ • • • • • • • • •

**4 oz Owl's Brew
Pink & Black**

2 fresh peach slices

1 oz mezcal

Fresh basil leaves

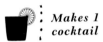

*Makes 1
cocktail*

Infuse the Pink & Black with the peach slices for 1 hour and 15 minutes. Remove the peach slices. You will only need 2 oz of infused Pink & Black for the cocktail, but you will lose some of the liquid when you remove the peach slices.

In a shaker, combine the infused Pink & Black, mezcal, and basil leaves. Muddle the basil, then shake with ice. Pour into a glass. Garnish with a basil leaf.

THE BITTER SUITE

Chocolate and coconut and mezcal—oh my!

• • • • • • • • • • • • • • • • • • • • • • • • • • •

3 oz Owl's Brew Coco-Lada

1 oz mezcal

Dash of chocolate bitters

In a shaker, combine the Coco-Lada, mezcal, and bitters. Shake with ice and pour into a glass.

 Makes 1 cocktail

BLACK + BLUE

Blackberry smoke.

← contributed by Chris Mitchell, Bubby's

. . . .

6–8 fresh blackberries

2 oz mezcal

1 oz Owl's Brew Coco-Lada

1 egg white

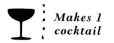 *Makes 1 cocktail*

In a shaker, muddle the blackberries. Add the mezcal, Coco-Lada, and egg white. Shake with ice. Strain and pour into a glass.

Chris invited us over one night to sample some new Owl's Brew cocktails. Five hours later, Black + Blue was the clear winner.

SMOKY MARGARITA

Tea and mezcal elevate a classic.

• • • • ✦ • • • ✦ • • ✦ • ✦ • ✦ • • • • • • • • • • • • •

Margarita salt

3 slices fresh jalapeño

2 oz Owl's Brew The Classic

1 oz mezcal

Before shaking, dampen the edge of the glass and coat the rim with salt. In a shaker, muddle the jalepeño. Add The Classic and mezcal. Shake with ice. Strain and pour into a glass.

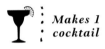

Makes 1 cocktail

We dreamed this up after a wonderful night sipping spicy mezcal cocktails at one of our favorite NYC cocktail joints, Mayuhuel.

LOWERED INHIBITIONS

contributed by Chris Mitchell, Bubby's

Cilantro smoke.

2 oz mezcal

1½ oz Owl's Brew Coco-Lada

½ oz lime juice

Dash of cilantro simple syrup (page 97)

1 lime slice

In a shaker, combine the mezcal, Coco-Lada, lime juice, and cilantro simple syrup. Shake with ice and pour into a glass. Squeeze in the lime slice.

Makes 1 cocktail

Another cocktail launched at our Owl's Hour program in the summer of 2014—we served our 500th cocktail to someone sipping Lowered Inhibitions.

BLACK + GINGER

Clean and spicy.

• • • • • ✓ ✓ ✓ ✓ ✓ ✓ ✓ • ✓ • • • • • • • • • • • • •

3 oz Owl's Brew Pink & Black (chilled)

1½ oz tequila

3 oz ginger ale

1 fresh ginger slice, for garnish

In a shaker, combine the Pink & Black and tequila. Shake with ice and pour into a glass. Top with the ginger ale and gently stir. Garnish with the fresh ginger.

Makes 1 cocktail

BASIL-RITA

An herbaceous tequila.

• • • • ✓ ✓ ✓ ✓ ✓ ✓ • ✓ • ✓ • • • • • • • • • • • • • •

5 fresh basil leaves

1 lemon slice

3 oz Owl's Brew The Classic

1½ oz tequila

In a shaker, muddle the basil leaves and lemon slice. Add The Classic and tequila. Shake with ice and pour into a glass.

Makes 1 cocktail

We served the Basil-Rita at a Self magazine happy hour—it was an editor favorite.

PINK TOMATO

Wake 'em and make 'em.

• • • • • ◦ • ◦ • ◦ • ◦ • ◦ • • • • • • • • • • • • • • •

5 oz tomato juice

1½ oz Owl's Brew
The Classic

1 oz tequila

1 oz red wine

2 dashes of
Worcestershire
sauce

2 dashes of hot
sauce

Pinch of celery salt

Ribs of celery,
for garnish

In a shaker, combine all of the
ingredients and shake with ice.
Pour into a glass. Garnish with
the celery.

*Makes 1
cocktail*

Pink Pom

PINK POM

Pretty in pink.

• • • • • ' ' • • • • • • • ' • • • ' • • • • • • • ' • • ' • • •

3 oz Owl's Brew Pink & Black

1½ oz tequila

½ oz pomegranate juice

In a shaker, combine the Pink & Black, tequila, and pomegranate juice. Shake with ice and pour into a glass.

 Makes 1 cocktail

THE ANTI-GRINGO

contributed by Chris Mitchell, Bubby's

For the love of spice.

• • • • ' ' • • • • • • • • ' • • • • ' • • • • • • • • • ' • • ' • • •

3 jalapeño slices

3 oz Owl's Brew Coco-Lada

1½ oz tequila

Dash of lime juice

1 lime slice, for garnish

In a shaker, muddle the jalapeños. Add the Coco-Lada, tequila, and lime juice. Shake with ice. Strain and pour into a glass. Garnish with the lime slice.

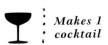 *Makes 1 cocktail*

THE CLASSIC SUNRISE

A sweet awakening.

• • • • ‚ • ‚ • ‚ ‚ ‚ • ‚ ‚ • • • • • • • • • • • • • •

**3 oz Owl's Brew
The Classic**

1½ oz tequila

½ oz orange juice

½ oz grapefruit juice

**1 grapefruit twist,
for garnish**

In a shaker, combine The Classic, tequila, orange juice, and grapefruit juice. Shake with ice and pour into a glass. Garnish with the grapefruit twist.

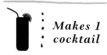

*Makes 1
cocktail*

MARGARI-TEA

Our spicy take on a margarita

. . . .

**3 oz Owl's Brew
The Classic**

1½ oz tequila

3 jalapeño slices

In a shaker, muddle the jalapeño.
Add The Classic and tequila. Shake
with ice. Strain and pour into a glass.

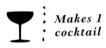

*Makes 1
cocktail*

In the mood for some spice?
Munch on our Lemongrass & Thai
Chile Tea Deviled Eggs (page 130)
while you sip your Margari-tea!

Lemongrass & Thai Chile Tea Deviled Eggs

contributed by Chris Mitchell, Bubby's

////////////////////////////////////

6 large eggs

3 tablespoons lemongrass tea leaves

1 fresh Thai chile, sliced open

3 lemons (juice and zest)

2 spicy pickles (finely chopped)

1 shallot (finely chopped)

½ cup mayonnaise

Salt

Leaves from ½ bunch basil, for garnish

Makes 12 deviled egg halves

Bring a pot of water to a boil. Boil the eggs for 12 minutes, and then transfer them to an ice bath to stop the cooking.

Bring 1½ quarts of water to a boil. Brew the lemongrass tea leaves and Thai chile in the water for 4 minutes. Strain, and let the tea cool.

Roll the eggs on the counter, cracking the shells but keeping them on. Place the rolled eggs in the tea overnight in the refrigerator to steep.

The following morning, carefully remove the eggshells to reveal the tie-dyed eggs. Cut each egg in half lengthwise and remove the yolk. Place the yolks in a bowl and add the lemon juice and zest, pickles, shallots, and mayonnaise. Mix to combine, season with salt, and spoon or pipe the mixture into the egg halves. Cut the basil leaves into chiffonade and garnish the eggs with the basil

OWL'S SHANDY

A tea spin on the classic shandy.

• •

5 oz Owl's Brew
The Classic (chilled)

5 oz wheat beer

1 orange slice,
for garnish

In a chilled glass, pour in The Classic
and top with the beer. Stir gently.
Garnish with the orange slice.

*Makes 1
cocktail*

THE HIGH NOON BREW

A cooldown with a kick.

• •

5 oz Owl's Brew
Coco-Lada (chilled)

5 oz light beer

1 lime slice,
for garnish

In a chilled glass, pour in the Coco-
Lada. Top with the beer. Stir gently.
Garnish with the lime slice.

*Makes 1
cocktail*

BREWLALA

A pink shandy.

• • • • ✓ • • ✓ • ✓ • ✓ • ✓ • • • • • • • • • •

1 lime wedge

Margarita salt

5 oz Owl's Brew Pink & Black (chilled)

5 oz lager

2 lime slices, for garnish

Run the lime wedge around the top of the glass, and then rim the glass with salt. Pour in the Pink & Black and lager. Gently swirl. Garnish with the lime slices.

Makes 1 cocktail

We seriously suggest that you serve this alongside the Sweet Tea-Brined Ribs (page 134).

Sweet Tea–Brined Ribs

contributed by CJ Bivona, chef

//

1 gallon brewed black tea

1 quart water

½ cup soy sauce

½ cup sugar

1 yellow onion (diced)

2 cloves garlic (smashed)

1 tablespoon black peppercorns

1 rack spare ribs (14–16 ribs)

Barbecue sauce

_____

Makes 1 rack ribs

Place the tea, water, soy sauce, sugar, onion, garlic, and peppercorns in a large pot, bring to a simmer, and simmer for 45 minutes.

Add the ribs to the pot, lower the heat, and simmer for 20 to 40 minutes, until the ribs are tender. Remove from the pot and let cool on baking sheets lined with parchment paper.

Fire up your grill and grab your favorite barbecue sauce. Char the ribs heavily on the grill until hot and cooked through. Brush generously with barbecue sauce and cook for 1 to 2 more minutes, until the ribs start to caramelize. Serve immediately.

ELDERFLOWER BREW

The saint's beer cocktail.

3 oz Owl's Brew
The Classic (chilled)

½ oz elderflower
liqueur

½ oz lemon juice

2 oz wheat beer

1 lemon twist,
for garnish

*Makes 1
cocktail*

In a shaker, combine The Classic,
elderflower liqueur, and lemon juice.
Shake with ice and pour into a glass.
Top with the beer and stir gently.
Garnish with the lemon twist.

A friend was looking
to class up a Super
Bowl party. We gave
him the recipe for
Elderflower Brew.

BOTANICAL BEER

Juniper hops.

• • • •• ′ ′ ′ ′ ′ ′ • ′ • • • • • • • • • • • • •

2 oz Owl's Brew Pink & Black (chilled)

1 oz gin

3 oz wheat beer

In a shaker, combine the Pink & Black and gin. Shake with ice. Strain and pour into a glass. Top with the beer and gently stir.

 Makes 1 cocktail

COCO BREW

A spiced beer.

4 oz Owl's Brew Coco-Lada (chilled)

4 oz stout beer (chilled)

In glass, pour in the Coco-Lada. Top with the beer. Gently swirl, if desired.

Makes 1 cocktail

We love this cocktail with a salty snack!

THE ROYAL BEER

A rich and robust classic.

• • • • ✦ ✦ ✦ ✦ ✦ • ✦ • ✦ ✦ • • • • • • • • • • • • •

**2 oz Owl's Brew
The Classic**

1 oz vodka

1 oz crème de cassis

5 oz wheat beer

In a shaker, combine The Classic, vodka, and crème de cassis. Shake with ice. Strain and pour into a glass. Top with the beer and gently swirl.

*Makes 1
cocktail*

This is one of our
go-to recipes for
summer BBQs.

SANGRITEA

Crowd-pleaser!

Fresh strawberries

Fresh raspberries

Orange slices

32 oz Owl's Brew Pink & Black

750ml white wine

In a pitcher, place the fresh fruit. Add the Pink & Black and wine. Gently stir. Chill for 1 hour and 15 minutes before serving or pour over ice and serve immediately.

Makes 60 oz

Outdoor Entertaining

HOSTING AN OUTDOOR GATHERING? HERE ARE A FEW TIPS!

✸ Serve your tea sangrias in oversize pitchers. The morning of your party combine the ingredients and let them sit all day. The longer the fruits and berries steep in your tea base, the more vibrant and delicious your cocktails will be!

✸ Mini mason jars are often the perfect glassware for an outdoor soiree.

✸ Striped straws add a delightful picnic vibe.

✸ Scribble a cocktail list on chalkboard menus for a homemade touch.

✸ Hoot, hoot! With all the time you've saved using Owl's Brew, come up with a few creative names for your specialty cocktails. Your guests will be impressed!

COCO SIPPER

Desser-tea!

2 oz Owl's Brew Coco-Lada (chilled)

2 oz lightly sweet white dessert wine (chilled)

Pour the Coco-Lada and wine into a glass. Gently swirl and sip!

 Makes 1 cocktail

THE WHITE CLASSIC ←

contributed by Chris Mitchell, Bubby's

Delicate and light.

1 peach, chopped

32 oz Owl's Brew The Classic

750ml dry white wine

4 oz Combier

½ pint fresh blueberries

In a pitcher, muddle the peach. Add The Classic, wine, and Combier. Add the blueberries. Gently stir. Chill for 1 hour and 15 minutes before serving.

 Makes 60 oz

Coco Sipper

BUBBLE BREW

An autumnal spin on the mimosa.

• • • • • ✦ • • • • • ✦ • • ✦ • • • • • • • • • •

3 oz Owl's Brew Coco-Lada (chilled)

3 oz Prosecco (chilled)

1 orange twist, for garnish

Pour the Coco-Lada into a glass. Top with the Prosecco. Gently swirl, if desired. Garnish with the orange twist.

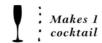 *Makes 1 cocktail*

If you are planning to sip the Bubble Brew for cocktail hour and you're looking for some delicious snacks to go along (we might be biased), we strongly urge you to try the Tea-Spiced Pecans. We promise they are tea-rrific!

Tea-Spiced Pecans

contributed by
Craig Koketsu, chef

//

4 cups raw unsalted pecan halves

2 cups Owl's Brew The Classic

1½ cups sugar

1½ teaspoons salt

½ teaspoon cayenne pepper

2 tablespoons Brew Lab black tea (or store-bought)

Canola or other neutral oil, for frying

Makes 4 cups

Place the pecans in a medium pot and add enough water to cover. Boil the nuts over high heat, about 2 minutes, and then drain in a strainer.

In another medium pot, combine The Classic, sugar, salt, and cayenne. Place over medium heat and bring to a simmer. Fill a tea linen or tea ball with the black tea and place in the pot to steep for about 2 minutes. Remove the sachet/ball and add the boiled pecans to the pot. Simmer the nuts in the syrup over medium heat for about 5 minutes. Drain. Let the nuts cool on an unlined metal baking sheet.

Heat a heavy pot with about 2 inches of oil to 350°F. Carefully place small batches of the pecans in the oil and fry for 3 to 5 minutes. Use a slotted spoon or wire mesh strainer to remove the nuts from the oil and transfer to a parchment-lined baking sheet. Let the nuts cool fully before serving.

Blackberry Bell

BLACKBERRY BELL

Fizzy and fantastic.

1 tablespoon fresh blackberries, plus a couple for garnish

3 oz Owl's Brew The Classic

3 oz Prosecco

In a shaker, muddle the blackberries with The Classic. Shake with ice and strain into a glass. Top with the Prosecco. Gently swirl, if desired. Garnish with blackberries.

Makes 1 cocktail

HIBISCUS BUBBLES

Tart and effervescent.

3 oz Owl's Brew Pink & Black (chilled)

3 oz Prosecco (chilled)

1 fresh strawberry, for garnish

Pour the Pink & Black into a glass. Top with the Prosecco. Gently swirl, if desired. Garnish with the strawberry.

Makes 1 cocktail

OLD FASHION OWL

An after-dinner indulgence.

• • • • ◦ ◦ • • • ◦ • ◦ • ◦ • ◦ • ◦ • • • • • • • •

3 oz Owl's Brew Coco-Lada

1½ oz brandy

1 oz fresh-pressed ginger juice

1 apple slice, for garnish

In a shaker, combine the Coco-Lada, brandy, and ginger juice. Shake with ice. Strain and pour into a glass. Garnish with the apple slice.

 : *Makes 1 cocktail*

BRANDY BREW

A sophisticated toddy.

• • • • ◦ ◦ • • • ◦ • ◦ • ◦ • ◦ • ◦ • • • • • • • •

3 oz Owl's Brew The Classic

1½ oz brandy

Honey, for garnish

In a saucepan, combine The Classic and brandy. Simmer over low heat for 8 minutes. Remove from the heat and pour into a heat-safe mug. Drizzle with honey for a sweet finish.

 : *Makes 1 cocktail*

Old Fashion Owl

TEA SODAS
AND *smoothies*

We say "Drink Wise!" because we believe you should know exactly what you are putting into your body—and, obviously, that it should be delicious! Our tea sodas and smoothies are perfect for adding some sparkly, nutrient-packed goodness to your daily routine.

Our tea-sodas use some no-brainer ingredients such as white tea and berries to deliver a sweet and vitamin C–packed punch. We also tap a few unsung botanical heroes, such as fennel and stinging nettle, to ramp up the health benefits in each blend.

Our tea-based smoothies offer a light, refreshing alternative to the typical yogurt or milk bases.

Chin-chin!

TART FIZZ

This unsweetened blend is incredibly refreshing, particularly on a hot summer day. Green rooibos contains natural electrolytes and is hydrating, while raspberries and lemon peel are rich in vitamin C.

• • • • • •   • • • • • • •   • • • • • • • • • • • • • • • • •

2½ teaspoons green rooibos

2½ teaspoons dried raspberries

1 teaspoon dried hibiscus flowers

Large pinch of dried lemon peel

5 oz sparkling water

Makes 1 soda

In a pitcher, place 10 oz of room temperature water. Add the green rooibos, raspberries, hibiscus flowers, and lemon peel. You can either use two tea linens or place the ingredients directly in the water and strain out after brewing. If you decide to use the tea linens, we like to place all the ingredients in a dry bowl to mix, and then evenly distribute into the linens.

Let the tea brew for 10 minutes, agitating from time to time. Remove the sachets or use a tea strainer to strain out the added ingredients.

Pour 5 oz of tea base into a glass and add in sparkling water. Serve over ice.

BERRY-BERRY BLAST

This vitamin C–packed drink is naturally sweet, while black tea adds a tiny caffeine kick.

2½ teaspoons black tea leaves

Mix together in equal parts and use 2½ teaspoons:

Dried blueberries

Dried blackberries

Dried strawberries

5 oz sparkling water

Makes 1 soda

In a pitcher, place 10 oz of room temperature water. Add the black tea, dried blueberries, dried blackberries, and dried strawberries. You can either use two tea linens or place the ingredients directly in the water and strain out after brewing. If you decide to use the tea linens, we like to place all the ingredients in a dry bowl to mix, and then evenly distribute into the linens.

Let the tea brew for 10 minutes, agitating from time to time. Remove the sachets or use a tea strainer to strain out the added ingredients.

Pour 5 oz of tea base into a glass and add in sparkling water. Serve over ice.

DETOX SODA

This cleansing blend balances the entire system, while licorice adds natural sweetness.

• •

1 teaspoon ground ginger

1 teaspoon dried licorice

1 teaspoon fennel seeds

1 teaspoon black pepper

1 teaspoon stinging nettle

5 oz sparkling water

Makes 1 soda

In a pitcher, place 10 oz of room temperature water. Add the ginger, licorice, fennel, pepper, and stinging nettle. You can either use two tea linens or place the ingredients directly in the water and strain out after brewing. If you decide to use the tea linens, we like to place all the ingredients in a dry bowl to mix, and then evenly distribute into the linens.

Let the tea brew for 10 minutes, agitating from time to time. Remove the sachets or use a tea strainer to strain out the added ingredients.

Pour 5 oz of tea base into a glass and add in sparkling water. Serve over ice.

WINTER SODA

This hydrating blend has anti-inflammatory properties, and ginger adds a healthy, spicy kick!

SIMPLE SYRUP
8 oz water
8 oz sugar

TEA BASE
1 teaspoon green rooibos
¾ teaspoon ground ginger
¾ teaspoon chopped dried apple
½ teaspoon fenugreek

TEA SODA
Tea base
1 oz simple syrup
6 oz sparkling water

Makes 1 soda

To make the simple syrup: Pour the 8 oz of water into a pan and bring to a boil. Once the water boils, immediately stir in the sugar until the mixture is clear. You'll use only 1 oz per soda.

You can either use a tea linen or place the green rooibos, ginger, apple, and fenugreek directly in the pan with the simple syrup.

Let sit for 1 hour, stirring from time to time. Remove the sachet or use a tea strainer to strain out the added ingredients. Let the mixture cool to room temperature.

Pour 1 oz of the tea base–infused syrup into a glass over ice. Add 6 oz of sparkling water and stir.

ROSEMARY & THYME

This blend boosts the immune system and calms the body.

SIMPLE SYRUP
8 oz water

8 oz sugar

TEA BASE
1½ teaspoons green rooibos

½ teaspoon dried rosemary

½ teaspoon dried thyme

½ teaspoon dried lemon balm

TEA SODA
Tea base

1 oz simple syrup

6 oz sparkling water

Makes
1 soda

To make the simple syrup: Pour the water into a pan and bring to a boil. Once the water boils, immediately stir in the sugar until the mixture is clear. You'll use only 1 oz per soda.

You can either use a tea linen or place the green rooibos, rosemary, thyme, and lemon balm directly in the pan with the simple syrup.

Let sit for 1 hour, stirring from time to time. Remove the sachet or use a tea strainer to strain out the added ingredients. Let the mixture cool to room temperature.

Pour 1 oz of the tea base–infused syrup into a glass over ice. Add 6 oz of sparkling water and stir.

PEACH VANILLA

Peach Vanilla contains natural mood enhancers and is rich in vitamin C.

SIMPLE SYRUP
8 oz water

8 oz sugar

TEA BASE
1½ teaspoons white tea leaves

½ teaspoon chopped vanilla bean

1 teaspoon dried peaches

TEA SODA
1 oz simple syrup

Tea base

6 oz sparkling water

 Makes 1 soda

To make the simple syrup: Pour the water into a pan and bring to a boil. Once the water boils, immediately stir in the sugar until the mixture is clear. You'll use only 1 oz per soda.

You can either use a tea linen or place the white tea, vanilla, and peaches directly in the pan with the simple syrup.

Let sit for 1 hour, stirring from time to time. Remove the sachet or use a tea strainer to strain out the added ingredients. Let the mixture cool to room temperature.

Pour 1 oz of the tea base–infused syrup into a glass over ice. Add 6 oz of sparkling water and stir.

THE GREEN AVOCADO

Yum! Wake up to a powerful body booster. Avocado is rich in healthy fats, lycopene, and beta-carotene. Lemon and lime add vitamin C, while green tea ups your metabolism.

TEA BASE

2 teaspoons pan-fired green tea

1 teaspoon chopped lemongrass

1 teaspoon dried peppermint

SMOOTHIE

8 oz brewed tea base

1 avocado (peeled and chopped)

1 tablespoon lime juice

1 tablespoon lemon juice

2 tablespoons agave nectar

In a cup, place 8½ oz of room temperature water.

In a tea linen or tea ball, combine the green tea, lemongrass, and peppermint. Brew in the room temperature water for 10 minutes, agitating from time to time. Remove the sachet/ball.

Add 8 oz of the tea base to a blender. Add the avocado, lime juice, lemon juice, and agave nectar. Blend until smooth.

Pour into a glass.

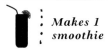

Makes 1 smoothie

TART IT UP

Rooibos is naturally hydrating and contains electrolytes, while the berries are rich in vitamins. Hibiscus is cleansing for the entire body.

TEA BASE
2 teaspoons green rooibos

1 teaspoon dried raspberries

1 teaspoon dried hibiscus flowers

½ teaspoon dried lemon peel

SMOOTHIE
8 oz brewed tea base

¼ cup frozen strawberries

¼ cup frozen blueberries

¼ cup frozen raspberries

In a cup, place 8½ oz of room temperature water.

In a tea linen or tea ball, combine the green rooibos, raspberries, hibiscus flowers, and lemon peel. Brew in the room temperature water for 10 minutes, agitating from time to time. Remove the sachet/ball.

Add 8 oz of the tea base to a blender. Add the frozen berries. Blend until smooth.

Pour into a glass.

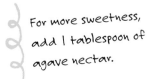

For more sweetness, add 1 tablespoon of agave nectar.

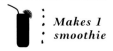

Makes 1 smoothie

MAPLE-VANILLA SMOOTHIE

Bananas and almonds provide enough energy to help you bounce through your morning. Kava kava calms the body, while vanilla is a mood enhancer.

TEA BASE
1 teaspoon green rooibos

½ teaspoon chopped vanilla bean

¼ teaspoon dried orange peel

¼ teaspoon fenugreek

¼ teaspoon kava kava

SMOOTHIE
8 oz brewed tea base

2 bananas (peeled and chopped)

¼ cup soaked raw almonds

1½ tablespoon maple syrup

In a cup, place 8½ oz of room temperature water.

In a tea linen or tea ball, combine the green rooibos, vanilla, orange peel, fenugreek, and kava kava. Brew in the room temperature water for 10 minutes, agitating from time to time. Remove the sachet/ball.

Add 8 oz of the tea base to a blender. Add the bananas, almonds, and maple syrup. Blend until smooth.

Pour into a glass.

Makes 1 smoothie

WAKE ME UP

A morning dose of vitamin C is perked up with the perfect amount of caffeine—a little goes a long way!

TEA BASE
1¼ teaspoons Assam tea leaves

Mix together in equal parts and use ¾ teaspoon:

Dried orange peel

Dried lemon peel

SMOOTHIE
8 oz brewed tea base

2 ripe mangoes (peeled and chopped)

1 cup fresh pineapple chunks or juice-packed pineapple chunks

2 teaspoons lemon juice

In a cup, place 8½ oz of room temperature water.

In a tea linen or tea ball, combine the Assam tea, orange peel, and lemon peel. Brew in the room temperature water for 10 minutes, agitating from time to time. Remove the sachet/ball.

Add 8 oz of the tea base to a blender. Add the mangoes, pineapple, and lemon juice. Blend until smooth.

Pour into a glass.

For more sweetness, add 1 tablespoon of agave nectar.

Makes 1 smoothie

ACKNOWLEDGMENTS

We would like to thank our families—Elizabeth Ripps, for her editing genius, as well as Jennie's mother, Susan, and brother for some keen reading. Our wonderful Brew Lab Tea and Owl's Brew Team—Joanna Brunner, Nina Lapenta, and Calli Nicoletti for their dedication and bravery (!) when sampling. For their wonderful recipes—Chris Mitchell, Walt Easterbrook, Lynnette Marrero, Josh Curtis, Bryan Schneider, Gates Otsuji, Kevin Denton, CJ Bivona, Warren Bobrow, and Elana Karp. The fantastic Rodale team—our editor, Dervla Kelly, as well as Mollie Thomas, Rae Ann Spitzenberger, Aly Mostel, and Emily Weber Eagan. From the Lisa Ekus Group, our excellent agent, Sally Ekus. And a big thank you to Amelia Ekus, who "discovered" us and brought our Brew home by way of a panna cotta. Our brilliant photographer—Tina Rupp, as well as our talented food and prop stylists, Chelsea Zimmer and Sarah Cave. To our extraordinarily talented graphic designer, Renata Sviridova. To our first tasters—Evan Ferrante, Eric DeCholnoky, and Sameer Gupta. Thanks to our owlet Juliet for the good cheer. And, of course—we'll always double down for Max and Marty.

We'd like to thank our champions—Frank Weil, Tom Moore, Tim Dunn, Michael Stillman, Devan Shah, Don Duberstein and his family. And, our intrepid friends and tasters, Rachel Messina, Mollie Charnas, Zach Michaelson, Erica Gianchetti, Josh Plotkin, Joyce Huang, Erin Frankel, Katie Aszklar, Donald Tsynman, Lauren Sercander, Jen Portland, Karen Knapstein, and Erin Edmison.

Finally, Jennie's dad, Richard Jay Ripps, who first taught

REFERENCES

Bryan, Lettice. *The Kentucky Housewife: Containing Nearly Thirteen Hundred Full Receipts*. Bedford, Mass: Applewood Books, 2000. Print.

Craddock, Harry, and Peter Dorelli. *The Savoy Cocktail Book*. London: Pavilion, 1999. Print.

DeGroff, Dale, and George Erml. *The Craft of the Cocktail: Everything You Need to Know to Be a Master Bartender, with 500 Recipes*. New York: Clarkson Potter/Publishers, 2002. Print.

Gascoyne, Kevin, François Marchand, Jasmin Desharnais, and Hugo Américi. *Tea: History, Terroirs, Varieties*. 2014. Print.

Griffiths, John. *Tea: The Drink That Changed the World*. London: Andre Deutsch, 2007. Print.

Haigh, Ted. *Vintage Spirits and Forgotten Cocktails: From the Alamagoozlum to the Zombie and Beyond: 100 Rediscovered Recipes and the Stories Behind Them*. Beverly, Mass: Quarry Books, 2009. Print.

Heiss, Mary Lou and Robert J. *The Story of Tea*. San Francisco: Ten Speed Press, 2007. Print.

Kappeler, George J. *Modern American Drinks*. New York: The Merriam Company, 1895 Reprint.

Mair, Victor H. & Roh, Erling. *The True History of Tea*. New York: Thames & Hudson. 2009. Print.

Martin, Laura C., Tea: *The Drink That Changed the World*. North Clarendon, VT: Tuttle Publishing, 2007. Print

Morgenthaler, Jeffrey, Martha Holmberg, and Alanna Hale. *The Bar Book: Elements of Cocktail Technique*. 2014. Print.

Pettigrew, Jane and Richardson, Bruce. *A Social History of Tea*. New York: Benjamin Press. 2014. Print.

Richardson, Lisa B. *Modern Tea: A Fresh Look at an Ancient Beverage*. San Francisco: Chronicle Books. 2014. Print.

Richardson, Lisa B. *Modern Tea: A Fresh Look at an Ancient Beverage*. 2014. Print.

Ross, Shirley. *Nature's Drinks; Recipes for Vegetable and Fruit Juices, Teas, and Coffees*. New York: Vintage Books, 1974. Print.

Stavely, Keith W. F. and Kathleen Fitzgerald. *America's Founding Food*. Chapel Hill, N.C.: University of North Carolina Press, 2004. Print.

Stewart, Amy. *The Drunken Botanist: The Plants That Create the World's Great Drinks*. Chapel Hill, N.C: Algonquin Books of Chapel Hill, 2013. Print.

Thomas, Jerry. *Bar-Tender's Guide: How to Mix Drinks*. 1862 Reprint. New York: SoHo Books. 2009. Print.

Tyree, Marion Cabell. *Housekeeping in Old Virginia*. Reprint 1879 Edition. Louisville,: KY: John P. Morton and Company. Creative Cookbooks, 2004. Print.

Waller, James. *Drinkology: The Art and Science of the Cocktail*. New York: Stewart, Tabori, and Chang, 2003. Print.

INDEX

Underscored page references indicate boxed text. **Boldfaced** page references indicate photographs.